Nations and Peoples

Portugal

Portugal

SARAH BRADFORD

with 30 illustrations and a map

WALKER AND COMPANY
NEW YORK

© Thames and Hudson Ltd. 1973

Library of Congress Catalog Card Number : 72-87516

ISBN 0-8027-2128-1

First published in the United States of America in 1973
by the Walker Publishing Company, Inc.

Printed and bound in Great Britain

Contents

	Preface	*page*	7
I	The individuality of Portugal		9
	Map of Portugal		13
2	Romans, Goths and Moors		24
3	The maritime era		31
4	The golden age of empire		38
5	Foreign domination		48
6	Absolutism and Enlightenment		53
	plates 1–16		57
7	The liberal era		65
8	The Republic 1910–26		73
9	Salazar and the New State		79
10	The last years of Salazar		84
11	Caetano's Portugal		88
12	Modernization and change		101
	plates 17–30		113
13	Portugal and the world		121

14 Society in the seventies   134

15 The future   149

    Notes on the text   160

    Acknowledgments   161

    Select Bibliography   161

    Who's Who   162

    Index   169

Preface

PORTUGAL is an enigmatic country, and the process of discovery enhances its fascination.

Most people will have heard of Vasco da Gama, Henry the Navigator, and Dr Salazar, but their ideas concerning Portugal and the Portuguese may be hazy or preconceived, and their experiences of the country limited to the beaches of the Algarve. Understanding Portugal today involves, perhaps to a greater extent than with any other nation, a knowledge of the racial and historical background. This book is intended to provide a short-cut to a country where history still impinges on everyday life.

The Portuguese are a small nation with a vast history; it is not surprising, therefore, that it should colour their instinctive attitudes to past and present. Professor Trevor-Roper has called the Portuguese the creators of the modern world; the early navigators were the astronauts of their day; their voyages symbolized man's conquest of the oceans in the fifteenth century much as the lunar missions represent his assault on space today. The knowledge of the existence and accessibility of distant continents, of diverse races, religions and civilizations, the concept of a wider world which resulted from their experiences, revolutionized Europe, breaking down the introverted attitudes of the Middle Ages and bringing it into the modern era.

Portugal has, therefore, an assured position in universal history, yet she has still to find her place in the modern world. Her economic and social development lags behind other continental nations, and her lack of a parliamentary system of government is seen as a hindrance to integration in the councils of Europe. Moreover she still retains vast territories in Africa where she maintains a large standing army that has been fighting a guerrilla war for over a decade.

Present-day Portugal is passing through a period of transition which makes this one of the most vital and fascinating epochs of her history, as significant for the nation itself as the voyages of discovery were for the outside world. What does the future hold for her ? Will she succeed in synchronizing a deeply traditional way of life with the rapid development of an increasingly integrated Europe ? Can she do this and yet conserve the essential qualities of her people ?

These are the questions facing Portugal today. In this book I have tried to present a picture of the Portuguese past and present, and to highlight the pervading themes and features, political, social and historical, which have a bearing on the life of the country today. I hope that it may contribute towards the understanding of a nation which remains the most individual in Europe.

London, 1972

1 The individuality of Portugal

PORTUGAL IS AN ISLAND in Europe. It is part of the continental land-mass and yet not of it; it is the western littoral of the Iberian peninsula, yet distinct from Spain which occupies four-fifths of the land area. Historical experience has divided Iberia from Europe; the concept 'Africa ends at the Pyrenees' has a basis in fact. Iberian civilization is the fusion of two cultures, the dominant strain from Europe inter-acting with the Arab heritage from North Africa. But if one talks of Iberian civilization and the Iberian peninsula, why is Iberia not a political entity? Looking at a map of the peninsula, the independent existence of Portugal appears illogical. The question arises – why Portugal? Yet if one takes a closer look at the geographical, cultural and historical factors which determined the country's evolution, the individuality of Portugal emerges.

Mainland Portugal is the south-western edge of Europe, the ultimate slope of an escarpment of the Iberian peninsula as it tilts downwards into the Atlantic. This Atlantic position has been one of the deciding factors of her destiny; the sea permeates Portuguese life, the proportion of her coastline to her total land area is three times the European average, and the greater part of the population live in the coastal areas. In shape the country is an inverted rectangular strip measuring some 350 miles from north to south, and between 70 and 140 miles in width, so that no part of Portugal is very far from the sea, while the climate generally is damper and milder than the arid extremes of the central Spanish *meseta*.

The seaward slope is the most important fact of the northern Portuguese landform; with her back to Spain and the mountains, Portugal is oriented towards the ocean. The polarizing effect of her long seaboard is enhanced by inland geographical features which determined her land frontiers with Spain. The eastern frontier area is mountainous, wild, barren, and sparsely populated. This seaward orientation of the land is most noticeable in the northern province of the Minho, which significantly was the original nucleus of the Portuguese kingdom. Here the mountains to the east, the Serras of Peneda, Gerez, Cabreira, Alvão, Marão, and Montemuro, form an amphitheatre facing the Atlantic. The bare mountains are infertile, inhospitable, in direct contrast to the rich lands stretching seaward, which represent one of the most densely populated areas of Portugal. This relative uninhabitability of the frontier area with its low rainfall, extreme climate, and barren, rocky soil, extends with few exceptions down the entire eastern boundary with Spain, from the province of Trás-os-Montes in the north-east to the southern province of Algarve. The distribution of population, dense on the coast, sparse in the frontier zones, which is the natural result of the physical structure of the land, has been one of the most important factors in the political separation of Portugal from Spain.

Rivers, which so often form channels of communication between peoples, have had the opposite effect between Spain and Portugal. They have served as boundaries in Iberia from time immemorial; when the Romans used them to define frontiers they were conforming to previous local custom. Sixty per cent of Portuguese land boundaries follow the lines of rivers, rising to over seventy per cent along the eastern border. In Trás-os-Montes the frontier rivers cut deep canyons in the old rocks of the plateaux, running through narrow, precipitous gorges. The Spanish Duero flows calmly westward to beyond Zamora until it becomes the frontier between Paradela and Barca d'Alva, when it runs through a canyon with vertical walls up to one hundred feet high for over seventy-six miles, dropping 1,600 feet over the distance. Beyond the frontier, the Portuguese Douro is unnavigable for boats of any size over most of its length. A series of dams is under construction which will change the level of the river, check its dramatic winter floods, and open it to navigation, but historically the Douro up to the Spanish border has been a violent, savage stream, a barrier rather than a channel of communication. Historically too, therefore, the impassability of the rivers at the border has turned the economic currents of the areas westward, away from Spain towards the lowlands; the population has drifted towards the coast, to the cities of the littoral, or to seek new opportunities overseas.

Most Portuguese rivers are only navigable for a short distance inland, a phenomenon that has become accentuated since the Middle Ages. This has been a not unimportant factor in the context of Portuguese independence. Although two of the country's major rivers, the Tagus and the Douro, both have their sources in central Spain, they have never, by reason of their impracticability, tempted the Spaniards to use them as paths to the Atlantic. One can only speculate as to what might have been the consequences had the Tagus been navigable from Toledo, only seventy kilometres from Madrid, down to Lisbon, one of the great natural harbours of the world.

Yet within its clear-cut frontiers, metropolitan Portugal, a small, compact country with a land area of 34,500 square miles and a population of some eight and a half million, has an amazing range of physical, cultural and climatic diversity. If, in midsummer, you were to take a plane from the northern frontier on the river Minho to the southern coastal province of Algarve you would see not one country but two: Atlantic and Mediterranean Portugal, the green patchwork fields of the north merging into an intermediate grey-green region of valleys and mountains in the centre of the country, with an abrupt change south of the Tagus to huge, open plains, the tawny, dusty earth of Africa and the central *meseta*.

The climate varies considerably from north to south; the Algarve has six dry months in summer, while the Minho has only two. Viana do Castelo at the mouth of the river Lima in the Minho receives sixty-one inches of rainfall in a year, while Lisbon in the centre of the country records twenty-four, and Faro, in the extreme south, less than sixteen. Frost is almost unheard of in Lisbon and Algarve, while snow falls every winter on the uplands of Beira and Trás-os-Montes. The vegetation varies with the climate: in the Atlantic north the maritime pine and the oak, both common to north-west Europe, are the dominant trees, while certain species of plants found in the north will not grow south of the river Mondego. South of the Mondego, Estremadura represents a transitional area: thirty-eight per cent of the plant species are those of north-western Europe (as compared with fifty-eight per cent north of the Mondego), and forty-two per cent belong to the Mediterranean. But Portugal south of the Tagus is closer to the Mediterranean and North Africa, only one-third of the species common to north-west Europe are found there, while the dominant trees are cork and holm oak (ilex), olive trees, both wild and cultivated, with the exotic, African touches of palms and carobs.

THE PROVINCES

Mainland Portugal is traditionally divided into twelve provinces: Minho, Trás-os-Montes, Douro, Douro Litoral and Beira Alta in the north; Beira Beixa, Beira Litoral, Estremadura, and Ribatejo in the centre; and Alto Alentejo, Baixo Alentejo and Algarve in the south.

At Caminha on the northern river frontier, the Minho, a gargoyle projects from the sixteenth-century parish church, making an extremely obscene gesture towards Spain. The fiercely independent nationalism it expresses is appropriate, for the Minho, once the ancient province of Entre-Douro-e-Minho, was the original nucleus of the Portuguese kingdom which declared its independence from Leon. Guimarães was the site of the first Portuguese court, and the birthplace of Afonso I, the first king of an independent Portugal, while Braga, once the capital of the Swabian kingdom, was the cradle of Portuguese Christianity, the metropole of the restored diocese after the reconquest of the territory from the Moors.

The Minho is the land of the *minifundia*, cottages surrounded by tiny patches of land, a smallholding system which descends from the time of the Swabian kingdom, as do its traditions of intensive cultivation. The Swabian ancestors of the *minhotos* were an essentially agricultural people, and their descendants are fanatically attached to the land, which they regard not so much as a source of production but as a cherished possession. Every inch of cultivable soil is cut up into minute holdings, the hereditary portions of different members of families, and each individual holding may consist of various strips of land which are not even contiguous.

Intensively cultivated and densely populated, the Minho has roughly twenty-three per cent of the population of Portugal on only eight per cent of the land. Traditionally it has been the source of emigrants who colonized the Portuguese world. The pressure of the population on the land sent waves of settlers southward to colonize the newly-won territories at the time of the Reconquest, and later to people areas of the Portuguese world overseas.

And yet the Minho is one of the most beautiful, fertile parts of Portugal, an idyllic landscape of green valleys with ancient manor

Map of Portugal

independent burgher tradition; in medieval times nobles were not allowed to reside within the city walls, and almost every liberal uprising throughout Portugal's history originated there. The *Portuenses*, nicknamed the *tripeiros*, the tripe-eaters, are noted for their gargantuan appetites and their capacity for work. They take themselves seriously and tend to regard southerners as idle layabouts; 'Braga prays, Coimbra studies, Lisbon plays, and Porto works,' runs an old saying. The same underlying antagonism exists between the northern industrial centre and the capital as between, say, Manchester and London.

Oporto is an anglicization of the Portuguese *o Porto*, which means 'the port'. Oporto gave its name to port wine in the seventeenth century, and the port-wine trade is still the *raison d'être* for a sizeable English colony, some of which have been resident there for generations. The wine is made in the High Douro country and matured in Vila Nova de Gaia across the river from Oporto in the stores, called 'lodges', of firms whose names may go back over three hundred years. Today Oporto is an expanding industrial area, centre of the flourishing textile industry, one of Portugal's major exports, brewing, oil refining, and manufacturing, with a busy port at Leixões, and one of the fishing and canning centres of the country at nearby Matosinhos.

South of Oporto, the Beiras are the farming heart of the country, relatively untouched by industrialization. The highest mountain range in Portugal, the Serra da Estrêla, separates the rich river valleys of the Vouga, Mondego and Dão from the bare frontier country to the east, as it divides the north of the country from the south. North-south communications run along the coast, or to the east up the fertile valley, the Cova da Beira, to Guarda. Fishing, centred on Aveiro and Figueira da Foz, arable farming, and wine-growing, especially in the Dão valley and the Bairrada area near Coimbra, are the chief occupations of the people. Coimbra, the most important town of this central region, is Portugal's third city in size, and is also the seat of her oldest university, whose buildings dominate the town.

In the early years of the Reconquest, Coimbra formed the southern bulwark of Portuguese territory, and the Muslim geographer al-Idrisi described its embattled inhabitants as 'the bravest of the Christians'. To the south, Estremadura was middle ground between Muslims and Christians for over a century, overrun by waves of invasion and counterinvasion, and sacked by raiding parties from both sides. It was resettled after the Reconquest under the Cistercian monks of Alcobaça, once the greatest monastery in the kingdom, and Estremadura has a claim to be called the religious heart of Portugal. It is the site of the two greatest abbeys, Alcobaça and Batalha, built by João I as a thank-offering for his victory over the Castilians at nearby Aljubarrota. Fátima, where the Virgin is believed to have appeared to three shepherd children in 1917, has the same significance in the religious life of the country as Compostela once had for Spain. It is a symbol of the rebirth of faith and the regeneration of the Portuguese Church, the re-awakening of the crusading spirit of Portuguese Christianity, the heritage of the struggle against the Moors, with Communism replacing Islam as the modern enemy of the Christian religion. Portugal is dedicated to Our Lady of Fátima, and the great pilgrimages to the shrine bring together thousands of Portuguese from all walks of life.

Estremadura, once the middle ground between Christian and Muslim, is a transitional area between north and south, where cultural, geographic and climatic elements mingle. Arab and Arabized topographic names, which are rare north of the Douro, are found there with Germanic place names inherited from the Swabian kingdom of the north, which are infrequent south of the Tagus. In climate, vegetation and agriculture it is the meeting ground between the Atlantic north and the Mediterranean south. Ox carts, rare south of Lisbon, begin in Estremadura; the trees take on a southern tinge. Apples, pears, walnuts and chestnuts grow beside peaches, almonds, figs, olives and oranges. Estremadura is a land of broken hills and winding valleys; the landscape has an indistinct character, and horizons are small until you reach the Tagus.

Lisbon, the capital on the Tagus (Tejo in Portuguese), is a blend of Africa and Europe, an essentially southern city. The huge sky to the south across the river, and the diamond clarity of the light, evoke North Africa, in direct contrast to the misty, rain-edged atmosphere of Oporto. There are palm trees in the gardens and jacarandas in the streets, and business hours are Mediterranean rather than northern European as they are in Oporto.

Lisbon's *raison d'être* was its superb natural harbour, and it is still a major port, as it was once the entrepôt of Europe in the days of the sixteenth-century spice trade with the East. Since the opening of the Straits of Gibraltar after the Christian conquest of Seville in the Middle Ages, Lisbon has been strategically situated on one of the world's major sea trade routes. It has been estimated that today some four hundred vessels per day pass along the Portuguese coast, and the closing of the Suez Canal and the era of the supertankers has increased her importance. Over three-quarters of Portugal's overseas commerce is seaborne, and a large proportion of it is handled through the port of Lisbon.

'Lisbon is Portugal!' exclaims one of Eça de Queirós' characters in *The Maias*, '... the entire country lies between the Arcade with its ministries and São Bento with its so-called parliament.' *The Maias* was written in the late nineteenth century, and the statement, although exaggerated, is perhaps even more true of the modern capital than it was in those pre-industrial days. As the centre of government, big business, overseas trade, and an expanding industry and tourism, the city exercises an increasingly powerful attraction over the rest of the country, and is the pole star for rural immigrants. Lisbon taxi-drivers, for instance, overworked and underpaid, are more often than not recently arrived immigrants from the provinces, a fact which accounts for the reckless abandon with which they tackle the traffic and the precipitous hills as if neither existed. In the wake of this accelerating expansion of prosperity and population, rents have rocketed despite the multiplication of new buildings over the past decade – hotels, offices, apartment blocks. In 1966, the mile-long Salazar suspension bridge was opened to link Lisbon with the south and the growing industrial zones across the Tagus: Barreiro, Margueira with a huge shipyard and dry dock, Seixal, site of the national steelworks, the *Siderurgia Nacional*. Perhaps nowhere else are the changes which are overtaking Portugal so apparent as they are in Lisbon – itinerant sellers still hawk their wares with hoarse, haunting cries, and gypsy women with their children in their arms beg in the shadow of multi-storey blocks.

In contrast to the capital, the Ribatejo east of Lisbon is one of the most traditional and Iberian of all the provinces. Seemingly endless flat fields stretch southwards under a vast empty sky; they are the *lezirias*, the bull-breeding grounds where mounted men, the *campinos*, in their distinctive dress, herd the fighting bulls. The river cuts the province into two regions which are as different from each other as if they were two continents : the north bank is intensely cultivated, with vines, maize and fruit trees, while to the south lie the open *lezirias* and rice paddies, the territory of the herdsman rather than the farmer. North of the river the province resembles Estremadura, and the great Convent of Christ at Tomar, once a stronghold of the Templars, ranks with the abbeys of Estremadura as a symbol of Portugal's history in stone. Beyond the *lezirias* to the south, the countryside with its cork oaks and sandy soil is indistinguishable from the neighbouring Alentejo.

Alentejo, 'beyond the Tagus', and the southern Ribatejo, 'the bank of the Tagus', are the lands of the *latifundia*, the great estates or *herdades*. These estates are the heritage of the Reconquest, when the medieval kings carved out great tracts of land, the donations, which they gave to the military orders, the Church and the nobles for resettlement and defence. The *herdades* or *latifundia* of the Alentejo represent the opposite extreme of the problem of the structure of Portuguese landholding to the *minifundia* of the Minho. Absentee landlords, unscientific use of the land, and an excessive dependence on traditional crops such as cork, olive oil and cereals are a feature of the Alentejo estates. Much of the territory, with the exception of the rich 'lands of Beja', appreciated by the Romans as a granary, is relatively infertile, with areas of cork forest and *charneca*, sandy heath. To the south round Elvas, Serpa and Estremoz, the vast olive groves remind one of Andalusia, and indeed the Alentejo, with its huge skies, open plains and extreme climate is the most Spanish of Portuguese provinces.

The Alentejo is one of the most sparsely-populated areas of Portugal. The people live not in villages and scattered small farms as they do in the rest of the country, but in towns spaced wide apart, or grouped on the semi-feudal *herdades*. For years the Alentejan agricultural workers were the lowest paid in the country, and there was serious seasonal unemployment due to the nature of the staple crops such as cork and olive products, which require labour at the harvesting period, but very little at other times of the year. However, conditions have improved considerably over the last decade as emigration and military service have produced a labour shortage, with its natural concomitants of sharp wage rises and more efficient farming. The scarcity and cost of labour has obliged even some of the more feudal landowners to use more scientific methods of cultivation, mechanization, and a more economic exploitation of their land. Eucalyptus, a fast-growing tree which feeds Portugal's expanding cellulose, pulp and wood industries, flourishes on the sandy, infertile soil of the province, and the ambitious irrigation scheme now under way under the Third Development Plan promises a better future for Alentejan agriculture. The government plans intensive farming areas there, producing export demand crops such as fruit and vegetables, on the lines of the agricultural pilot schemes in operation in Spain near Badajoz.

Cut off from the Alentejo by the mountains of Caldeirão and Monchique, the southernmost province of Algarve is quite unlike the Alentejo, even less like the northernmost province, Minho. It is the most Arab of the regions, and was the last to be conquered from the Moors; its late adherence to the body of Portuguese territory was implicit in the royal title: the sovereigns were 'kings of Portugal and of the Algarve'. As such it represents one of the poles of Portuguese culture, the Moorish south, as opposed to the Swabian Celtic north. The Moors settled densely in the Algarve, which they found most resembled North Africa, and left their stamp deeply imprinted on the agriculture, fishing, customs, and architecture of the region. The orange groves, figs, almonds and palm trees, the white cottages blazing in the sun with their chimneys curiously fretted like minarets, give the area an exotic African flavour.

Once a rustic province of farmers and fishermen, the Algarve has boomed as a tourist area over the last ten years. Its advantages are good beaches, a warm, equable climate, backed by an attractive countryside, and above all the strenuous efforts of the Portuguese government to prevent it from being spoiled by uncontrolled development.

Algarve faces Africa, a reminder that much of Portuguese territory still lies overseas. Under the ideology of Salazar's unitary corporative state, Portugal is 'one from the Minho to Timor', and in terms of population and land area, the overseas, *Ultramar*, far outweighs the home country. Portuguese territory today includes metropolitan Portugal – the mainland and the Atlantic archipelagoes, Madeira and the Azores – and the overseas provinces: Angola and Guiné (Portuguese Guinea) on the west coast of Africa, the Cape Verde islands off the Guinea coast, the equatorial islands of São Tomé and Principe, and Mozambique on the East African coast. Together they represent nearly seven per cent of the total land area of Africa and, with a total population of slightly over thirteen million, just under five per cent of its people. In Asia, Portugal retains the toehold she gained in China over four centuries ago at Macau – Portuguese since 1556 – and Timor in the Indonesian archipelago. Madeira and the Azores are administered as districts of the mainland, while the African and Asian territories have the status of overseas provinces and are governed through the Overseas Ministry. Of her former empire, Goa, Damão and Diu were occupied by India in 1961, although they are still officially regarded as Portuguese, and Brazil, discovered in 1500, declared her independence in 1822.

Mainland Portugal, despite its small size, is a country of physical diversity. Each province has its own distinctive characteristics, geography and way of life; only 'the Beiras' of the centre share many common features. Many of these different regions of Portugal bear closer resemblance to certain Spanish provinces than to other Portuguese areas. The hot, open plains of the southern Alentejo, bounded by mountains under a wide sky, dotted with cork trees or silver with olive groves, are far more like Andalusia or Spanish Extremadura than they are like the Portugal of the centre or the north. The north-western Spanish province of Galicia resembles the Minho far more closely than it does any other Spanish region, and the Galician dialect is more closely related to the Portuguese than to the Castilian.

Yet for all its physical diversity, Portugal has always been a remarkably compact country, and despite strong provincial loyalties it has never shown the centrifugal, separatist tendencies which have plagued other European nations. This is certainly partly due to its small size, but also to the all-important fact of its early historical development as an independent kingdom, which gave it stable land frontiers within which to develop a sense of nationality and unity of purpose, and to mould people of different cultures and experience into a homogeneous group – the Portuguese.

THE PEOPLE

Who then are the Portuguese? 'The Portuguese is a Spaniard with his back to Castile and his eyes on the Atlantic ocean,' wrote Salvador de Madariaga, showing a profound misunderstanding of the Portuguese character only too common among their Iberian neighbours. Common traits derived from shared historical, cultural and – for a brief space – political experience can be misleading. It is the differences, not the similarities, between the two nations that are the most characteristic of each.

The Portuguese are predominantly an Atlantic not a Mediterranean people. Although they like to describe themselves as Latins, their temperament has very little in common with that of, say, the Italians. They are on the whole introverted, quiet, reserved, where the true Latin is an extrovert. The Italian phrase *far bella figura* has no equivalent in Portuguese, and indeed the Portuguese has a horror of making a spectacle of himself, a quality that belongs to the north of Europe rather than the south.

Successive visitors to Portugal have remarked on the sadness, the Atlantic melancholy, of their expressions, and if there is one quality that is totally, untranslatably Portuguese it is contained in the word *saudade*. *Saudade*, or rather, *saudades*, is a state of longing for a person or a place, a bitter-sweet feeling something akin to the ancient Greek word *pothos*. Or it can be an inexplicable mood of sadness, not to be confused with depression. '*Estou triste hoje*', 'I'm feeling sad today', is a common expression among the people. But sadness, *tristeza*, as opposed to *saudades*, is only a passing mood. Normally the Portuguese like to laugh, and one of the most popular radio programmes is the lunch-time comedy hour. In a country with a strong oral tradition and a censored press, jokes play an important rôle as topical comment on the figures, trends and attitudes of the day. 'Have you heard this one?' is a frequent beginning to a conversation.

Nonetheless, an 'absurd desire to suffer' as the poet Cesário Verde described it, is a definite part of the Portuguese character, closely linked with *saudades*. *Saudosismo*, a sense of loss, of things past that will never return, is a recurrent theme in history and literature. 'What do you want of me, perpetual *saudades*?' wrote Camões, Portugal's greatest poet. 'With what hope are you still deceiving me? For time past will never return, and if it did, I should no longer be the age to enjoy it.'[1]

The Portuguese have a strong, often too strong, sense of the past; the great nineteenth-century liberal historian, Alexandre Herculano, wrote of Portugal as laden down with the weight of her history. An American commentator who met Dr Salazar in 1963[2] described him as 'profoundly absorbed by a time dimension quite different than our own, conveying the strong yet curious impression that he and his whole country were living in more than one century, as though Prince Henry the Navigator, Vasco da Gama and Magellan were still active agents in the shaping of Portuguese policy.' It is this sense of history, of their country's historic rôle in the shaping of the modern world which the era of the Discoveries represented, which lies beneath their attitude to their overseas territories, and contributes to their intense patriotism. It is less strong in the young generation, who are more oriented towards Europe of the seventies than Portugal of the fifteenth century, but it remains an important part of the Portuguese make-up.

A time dimension in which present and past are fused is a feature of the Celtic character, which the Portuguese derive from their Celtic ancestors and share with other Celtic peoples like the Irish. Combined with the fatalism which they have inherited from their Islamic past, it has often produced an attitude of passivity in the face of events. 'It was not worth taking one step to reach anything on this earth,' declared one of the characters in *The Maias*, 'because everything resolved itself... in dust and disillusion.' Lack of persistence can be a Portuguese weakness; fiery enthusiasms are followed by apathy in the case of disappointments, induced by this strong sense of fatalism and a certain lack of self-confidence.

Yet, conversely, the Portuguese are incredibly brave and patient in the face of elemental things they understand – the sea, poverty, hunger. Anyone who has read the chronicles of the exploits of the Portuguese overseas in the fifteenth and sixteenth centuries, the journeys of ordinary men like Pero de Covilhã and Fernão Mendes Pinto, cannot but be struck by their physical courage and fortitude in the face of enormous odds. The odds never made any difference to them when they were convinced they were right; and in such circumstances they can be extraordinarily tenacious, as they have shown themselves to be in the defence of their African territories over the past decade.

In the same way they are fiercely loyal to anyone they accept as a friend and thus exceptionally hurt by betrayals. They have an intensely personal, direct way of looking at things – despite an Oriental love of intrigue for its own sake – and a basic human kindness with a tendency to sentimentality. *Coitadinho*, 'poor thing', is one of the most overworked words in the language. *Bondade*, goodness in the sense of a good person not a prig, and *humanidade*, humanity, are qualities which the Prime Minister, Marcello Caetano, has called 'the greatest richness' of the people.

A French writer included these qualities among 'those individual features of the Portuguese soul which so clearly distinguish her from her Peninsular neighbours'. 'On the one side,' he wrote, 'a proud, exalted people, ready for every sacrifice and violence which their preoccupation with their dignity (*pundonor*) could inspire them; on the other side more melancholy and more indecision, more sensibility to the charm of children and women, a true humanity which is one of the most precious treasures of the patrimony of our old western Europe.'[3]

To understand the individuality of Portugal and the Portuguese one must go back to the roots of her history. Portugal became an independent nation early in comparison with other European states, two centuries before Castile completed the unification of Spain, and she has maintained her national unity and territorial integrity to a unique degree. She has the oldest land-locked frontiers in Europe; a fact which partially explains her homogeneity as a nation. The early emergence of Portugal as a territorial entity distinct from Spain, and her maintenance of her independence, are the salient facts of her existence as a nation. The question of why and how Portugal and the Portuguese became what they are, of how they achieved their individuality, is a question of history.

2 Romans, Goths and Moors

'TO THE NORTH of the Tagus', wrote Strabo, Greek historian of the Augustan age, 'stretches Lusitania, inhabited by the most powerful of the Iberian peoples, who resisted the arms of Rome for the longest period.' Rome created Lusitania, the land that was to become Portugal; Roman arms and administrative genius welded together the scattered tribes of the western Peninsula, and gave them a territorial identity.

The Lusitanians, described by Strabo, were a Celt-Iberian tribe inhabiting the mountainous country between the Tagus and the Douro. They greased their bodies, took primitive sauna baths, and ate once a day in common. They were sober, monogamous, wore their hair long and were fond of dancing. They were also savage and warlike, sacrificing captives to Ares, while their priests read the omens from the entrails of living victims. For fifty years from 193 BC they held up the advance of Rome, led by Viriatus, the Iberian Vercingetorix. After Viriatus' death by treachery in 139 BC, resistance was confined mainly to the north where the Lusitanians retreated to fortified hilltop settlements, the *castros*, but fighting continued sporadically until about 19 BC when Hispania was considered to be pacified under Augustus.

The Augustan reorganization of the province of Lusitania had an important influence on the form of the future kingdom. Lusitania was separated from Galicia, and stretched from the Douro in the north to the Algarve in the south. Although it included Salamanca, Toledo, and Mérida, the capital, to the east, the principal road system, a factor of prime importance in the physical unification of the province, ran in a dorsal line from north to south.

Over seven centuries the Romans imposed a cultural, linguistic, administrative and religious unity on the western Peninsula. They

24

brought the native peoples down from their embattled *castros* to cultivate the richer lowlands, taught them the use of the plough, planted grapes and made wine. Roman Lusitania produced linen, woollen cloth, preserved fish, dyes, and horses which were famous for their speed and stamina. The Romans created an urban civilization where none had existed before, introduced a common administrative and legal system and the use of Latin as the official language. Local tribal religions were absorbed into the imperial cult, which was later superseded by the uniquely unifying force of Christianity.

Roman Lusitania was a marginal province of the great Empire, remote on the shores of the western ocean, and her provincialism is reflected in the monuments that have survived: moderate-sized towns such as Conimbriga, the simple temple of Diana at Évora, bridges, rustic villas. But Portugal inherited from Rome her language, the Christian religion and the Mediterranean way of life in urban civilization and agriculture. Roman influence was particularly strong south of the Tagus in the Alentejo, where even today the pattern of occupation – the towns, the vast *herdades* corresponding to the *latifundia*, and the isolated farms, *montes*, the equivalent of the *villa rustica* – reflect the Roman heritage.

The Roman era came to an end early in the fifth century, when groups of barbarian Gothic tribes from Germany crossed the Pyrenees. Of these the Swabians settled in northern Portugal, where Roman influence had been weakest and native Celtic traditions more enduring. Their kingdom, with Braga as its capital, stretched from Cantabria to the Tagus and included Galicia. The Swabians were not innovators; primarily a pastoral people, they adopted Roman institutions much as they found them, and were eventually converted to Christianity. The upper classes spoke Latin, and only forty terms in Portuguese today can be traced back to the Gothic.

The Swabian kingdom was eventually absorbed by the Visigothic monarchy which ruled Iberia from Toledo, and became involved in its final downfall. The Visigothic tradition of elective monarchy led to an endless succession of dynastic quarrels, until in 711 the defeated faction invited the militant· power of Islam to cross the Straits of Gibraltar. The invading Muslims sacked Toledo and swept through the Peninsula; the Visigothic kingdom crumbled before them. Within ten years of their landing at Algeciras, the Moors controlled Iberia.

Moorish dominion of Portugal was destined to last five centuries. As in the case of Roman Lusitania, the Muslim provinces of the western Peninsula were remote from the great cultural and political centres of Andalusia, and the few surviving monuments of the period, the mosque at Mértola, the castle at Sintra, cannot be compared with the magnificence of Cordova, Granada and Seville. Nonetheless, Moorish influence on the life and language of the people was strong and enduring.

In agriculture the Moors reinforced the Mediterranean ways inherited from the Romans; they introduced lemons, oranges, probably also rice, and developed the culture of the olive; they planted orchards and developed irrigation, and the traditional Moorish form of intensive cultivation round the principal cities can still be seen in the vicinity of Silves, Faro, Setúbal and Lisbon.

Their influence was strong in fishing and shipbuilding; the *copejo* method of tunny fishing still in use in the Algarve is an Arab legacy, as is the shape of many Portuguese fishing boats. Silves had a flourishing shipyard in the Muslim era, and some historians have suggested that a small Arab boat called the carib was the prototype of the famous fifteenth-century caravels of the Portuguese navigators. In architecture, Islamic traditions and construction in carpentry, metalworking, masonry and decoration lasted well into the sixteenth century and never entirely disappeared.

Six hundred words in the Portuguese vocabulary derive from the Arabic. They relate principally to agriculture, but also to commerce, shipbuilding, social organization and everyday domestic life. Muslim society centred on the cities; they were great merchants and traders and skilled artisans. Idrisī, an Arab geographer writing in 1154, noted that all the wealthy centres of commerce in the western Peninsula, Faro, Silves, Évora, Alcácer, Santarém and Elvas, were in the Muslim dominions, and that in the Christian territories only Compostela could compare with them; after the Christian reconquest early overseas trade was largely limited to continuing or reviving that which had previously existed under the Moors. Undoubtedly Muslim skills in geography, astrology and navigation played a part in the later development of Portugal as a maritime nation.

Despite the triumph of Christianity, centuries of coexistence instilled certain Arab traits in the Portuguese make-up, among them a strong sense of fatalism and a basically Oriental attitude to the seclusion of women. Muslim dominion and its consequences distinguished the Iberian experience from that of the rest of Latino-Christian Europe.

THE RECONQUEST

The process of Christian reconquest of territory from the Moors was, after the formation of Roman Lusitania, the second vital stage in the evolution of Portugal. It determined not only the physical shape of the future kingdom, but also the organization and composition of its society. The experience of wresting national territory, 'God's patrimony', from the infidel, and the consequent identification of national security with religious orthodoxy, left an indelible impression on Portuguese psychology. Iberian Christianity gained a crusading intolerance which it never entirely lost, and the spirit of the *Reconquista* was to be a recurrent theme in Portuguese history.

The emergence of the Christian Portuguese kingdom has to be seen against a background of alternating pressure between Christians and Muslims. The pattern regularly consisted of drives from the Christian north at times when Muslim power to the south was in a state of confusion through internal dissension, followed by renewed invasion of Christian territory by militant groups recently arrived from Africa.

North of the river Mondego, and specifically north of the line of the Douro, the Muslim presence was scarcely apparent. The Moors settled mainly south of the Tagus, and particularly in the Algarve, content to leave the administration of the northern areas to local Visigothic nobles, and maintaining only scattered Berber garrisons. It was, naturally, from the north that the first Christian offensive came: a Visigothic noble, Pelayo of Asturias, defeated a force of Berbers at Covadonga in the second decade of the eighth century. His grandson, Alfonso, recovered Galicia from the Muslims, and in 868 a Galician, Vimara Peres, occupied the line of the Douro and rebuilt the old Swabian stronghold of Portucale (Oporto).

Portugal was created round Portucale: the surrounding territory, the *Territorium Portugalense*, was resettled, and by the end of the century included all the land between the Douro and Minho rivers. By the tenth century it was a feudal county subject to the kingdom of Leon, and by 1097, when Alfonso of Leon granted the '*Portu-*

calensis Provincia' to Count Henry, cousin of the Duke of Burgundy, the feudal county stretched as far south as the river Mondego. These early territorial gains were the results of Christian drives against Muslim weakness during the confused period after the break-up of the unity of the Caliphate of Cordova, and Alfonso's grant to Count Henry was a reward for his services against a fierce Muslim counterattack in 1093.

Count Henry married one of Alfonso's bastard daughters and set up court at Guimarães as a vassal of Leon. The County of Portugal, though linked with Galicia by language, began to take on a separate existence, grouped round three centres: the court at Guimarães, Braga, the metropole of the restored diocese, and Porto, the port; Coimbra was the southern bulwark of Christianity, launching point for raids into Muslim territory. The County was described by Idrisī as a fertile and populous land of rivers, castles, orchards and villages.

Such was the feudal fief inherited by Henry's son, Afonso Henriques, on his father's death in 1112. Afonso Henriques, later Afonso I, was the founder of the Portuguese kingdom and the first monarch of the Burgundian dynasty. His territories were bounded to the north and east by the powerful kingdom of Leon and Castile; the only opportunity for expansion lay to the south against the Muslim lands. Taking advantage of a power struggle among the Muslims, he drove south towards the Tagus. In 1139 he won the battle of Ourique near Santarém, threw off his vassal status and took the title of King. In 1147, when the Moors were occupied with the defence of Seville against Alfonso VII of Castile and Leon, he captured Lisbon. By the end of his reign in 1185, his kingdom included Évora and Beja in the Alentejo. Over the comparatively short period of one hundred and fourteen years under the first five kings of the Burgundian dynasty, Portugal attained her territorial limits. With the fall of Faro, the last Moorish stronghold in the Algarve, in 1249, the Christian reconquest of Portugal was complete.

In Spain, however, the process was more long drawn out, ending only in 1492, over two hundred years later, with the capitulation of Granada. The continuing preoccupation of the Castilian kings with their own drive against Islam preserved the nascent Portuguese kingdom from attack by her powerful neighbour and former suzerain. Castilian strength and Muslim weakness, and above all the combination of territorial ambition with crusading Christianity which the struggle against Islam represented, determined the physical development of the Portuguese kingdom.

The consequences of Muslim dominion and the circumstances of the Reconquest influenced the organization and composition of the new society. There were great differences between the fertile, populous County of Portugal which had known a long period of peace since the eighth century, and the lands south of the Mondego which had been the battleground during one hundred and fifty years of struggle between Christians and Muslims. The early kings were faced with the problems of resettlement and defence as they expanded their territory southward. Their solution of these problems affected the system of landholding in the centre and south of the country, contributed greatly to the power and wealth of the military Orders, the barons and the Church, and influenced the development of municipal freedoms.

Vast areas of the centre and south were granted in donations by the Crown to the Church – the Cistercian monastery of Alcobaça was responsible for the colonization of Estremadura – to the military Orders, the Templars at Tomar, the Hospitallers at Crato, the Order of Calatrava at Évora, and the Knights of Santiago at Palmela who alone controlled more than a third of the land south of the Tagus. Charters and land were granted to already existing towns, while land-hungry colonists from the overpopulated north were given royal charters to form municipalities, and in the frontier regions areas immediately surrounding castles were demarcated as *coutos de homiziados* where criminals could live with impunity.

Portuguese society after the Reconquest was a racial and linguistic mixture, a fusion of two cultures – the Gothic (Galaico-Portuguese) north with the Romano-Moorish (Mozarab) south. While the southerners spoke Arabic and a southern dialect of the Romance, the northerners spoke a Romance which had evolved within the unity of the old Swabian kingdom which had included Galicia. The Galaico-Portuguese influence from the north imposed itself on the Mozarab, and Romanesque architecture spread south with the Reconquest – the cathedrals of Coimbra, Lisbon and Évora belong to this period. The fusion and interaction of these distinct ethnic, cultural and linguistic strains created the individuality of the new Portuguese nation.

Although the northern influence predominated in the social and cultural evolution of the new kingdom, the Mozarabs, the Christian Romano-Visigothic population formerly living under Moorish rule, were numerous. In Lisbon at the time of the city's capture in 1147, at least half of the population were Mozarabs and they had their own bishop. After the first revengeful fury of the Reconquest had died down, Muslims, *mouros*, living under Christian rule were treated in much the same way as the Moors had treated the Mozarabs. They were tolerated, but discriminated against, socially and financially. Although allowed their own officials, courts, schools and places of worship, they were obliged to live in ghettoes, *mourarias*. They were totally subject to the king, who referred to them as 'my Moors', and they paid dearly for his protection with an onerous system of tributes. Yet although sexual intercourse between Christian and infidel was forbidden on pain of death, both Afonso I and his grandson Afonso III had bastards by Muslim women, and discrimination during the early Middle Ages was certainly less ferocious than it was later to become.

Portuguese territorial unity had been achieved within an amazingly short time. Within the space of just over one hundred and fifty years, Portugal, once dominated with the rest of the Peninsula by Romans, Visigoths and Moors, had emerged as an independent kingdom – two centuries before Castile finally completed the unification of Spain. By the end of the thirteenth century she had achieved a stable land frontier within which the cultural, racial and religious mixture could develop into a nation. Rome, Islam, and crusading Christianity had made their contributions to the emergence of Portugal; it was now up to the Portuguese to determine their destiny.

3   The maritime era

IN THE EARLY MIDDLE AGES Portugal was a small country on the western fringe of Europe, isolated, cut off from the centres of commerce and civilization in northern Europe and the Mediterranean. 'The Atlantic littoral', wrote a Portuguese historian, 'implies a destiny, both contradictory and alternating, of isolation and distant maritime relations.'[1]

In the centuries immediately following the Reconquest, Portugal turned towards the Atlantic and became a maritime nation. The consequences of this evolution were to be incalculable both for herself and for the rest of Europe. Within 250 years of the fall of Faro, the Portuguese became possessed of the first and the greatest seaborne empire the world had yet seen. How and why did this small, relatively poor nation embark on this great venture?

Geographically, Portugal's maritime destiny was predictable; a nation with such a long coastline in relation to its land area would inevitably be attracted towards the sea. Moreover, in the early Middle Ages the coast was more deeply indented than in modern times, and the rivers were navigable for a considerable distance inland; there were more natural harbours, twice as many ports as there are today. Once the seas were cleared of Muslim pirates after the taking of Lisbon, the natural movement of the population towards the coast was accelerated.

The importance of the rivers and the coast as a means of communication and trade were enhanced by the position in which Portugal found herself in the century immediately following the Reconquest. To the south the Muslims blocked the path to the Mediterranean, then the chief entrepôt for the luxury trade with the Orient. To the north and east the hostile power of Castile and Leon straddled the

31

overland routes to the commercial centres of northern Europe. Trade with England, the cities of the Hanseatic League, and the great Flanders entrepôts had of necessity to be seaborne.

Already in the twelfth century Portuguese merchants were engaged in the Flanders trade and had a factory in Bruges; by the thirteenth they were resident in London, Seville and several French ports. They traded principally in wine and salt, followed by fruit, dried fish, honey, wax, hides and wool, in exchange for woollen cloth, spices, arms, precious metals and luxury goods. Portugal's overseas commerce increased rapidly during this period. The early unification of the country and its political stability laid a firm basis for expansion, but it was the opening of the Straits of Gibraltar after the Christian conquest of Seville in 1248 which provided the vital stimulus. Seaborne communications between the nations of northern Europe and the rich Mediterranean entrepôts were made possible for the first time since the Roman era, and the importance of Portuguese harbours, strategically sited on this vital trade route, was vastly increased.

The Burgundian kings played their part in the encouragement of maritime commerce. Dinís (1279-1325) planted the great pine forest of Leiria, the Pinhal do Rei, to provide timber for shipbuilding, equipped a fleet and engaged the Genoese Emmanuele Pessagna as admiral to counter the activity of Barbary pirates on the Portuguese coasts. Fernando I (1367-83) stimulated native commerce, protected Portuguese traders from foreign competition, and set up a fund for the insurance of merchant shipping.

By the end of the fourteenth century Portugal was one of the leading maritime nations of Europe, and Lisbon one of the principal ports. King, nobles, merchants and clergy took part in a flourishing overseas trade, and the chronicler Fernão Lopes estimated that in the 1350's as many as four to five hundred ships might lie at anchor in the Tagus, of which not more than half would be Portuguese. A considerable foreign colony gave the city a cosmopolitan character, a mingling of English, Lombards, Bretons, Provençals, Flemings, and above all the Genoese, who with their nautical skills and their knowledge of the use of charts and the compass were to play a part in the voyages of discovery. The foundations for the maritime adventure of the fifteenth century were already laid.

At the dawn of the fifteenth century Portugal enjoyed two invaluable advantages over most other European nations: internal peace and freedom from external threat. The Burgundian dynasty, descendants of Afonso Henriques, produced several energetic and competent kings, notably Afonso III (1246-79), Dinís, and Pedro I (1357-67). It was on the whole a popular monarchy; the first parliament, the Cortes of Leiria in 1254, included delegates of the people, *procuradores do povo*, and the merchant and popular classes tended to support the kings in their efforts to curb the pretensions of the nobles and the Church. With the expansion of commerce the number of chartered municipalities and the importance of the mercantile class increased. In 1353 the merchants of Lisbon and Oporto independently negotiated an important commercial treaty with Edward III of England, which was signed on their behalf by an Oporto merchant. The same period saw the rise of a new educated middle class of clerks and lawyers, *letrados* and *legistas*, on whom the kings relied for the royal administration.

This social unity was reinforced by the success of the so-called popular revolution of 1383, which ended the threat from Spain and founded the alliance with England. Fear of Spanish territorial ambitions was ever-present during the fourteenth century and the fear became a reality when in 1383 Fernando, the weak last king of the Burgundian dynasty, died leaving as heiress to the throne of Portugal his only daughter Beatriz, married to Juan I of Castile.

The people rose against the pro-Spanish regency of the Queen, Leonor, and her Galician lover, the Conde de Ourém. The revolt was engineered by a *letrado*, Álvaro Pais, and headed by João, Master of the Order of Aviz, the bastard brother of the late king. It was a popular, urban movement, organized by the four great municipalities of the kingdom, Lisbon, Oporto, Coimbra and Évora. At Coimbra in 1385 the *cortes* declared João king and defender of the realm, and at the battle of Aljubarrota in the same year the Castilians were decisively defeated.

The reign of João I marked the apogee of the power and influence of the popular urban classes; at the Coimbra *cortes*, the representatives of the municipalities, the *concelhos*, presented a list of those whom they wished nominated to the royal council, which, when chosen, consisted of one prelate, two *fidalgos* (nobles), three *letrados* and four citizens. They also called for the annual convocation of *cortes*. João presided over a·united country; only the older nobility had fought for Castile, many of their sons had supported the revolution, and the higher and lower clergy, with few exceptions, had sided with the Master of Aviz.

Freed from the threat of absorption by Castile, and purged of dissident elements, Portugal was a dynamic, united, outward-looking nation, ready for the great adventure the next century was to bring forth. She had a sizeable merchant fleet, the technical knowledge gained from practical experience, a system of marine insurance, and credit resources, derived from the foreign banking houses established in Lisbon, to finance overseas enterprise. While the other countries of Europe, including her Spanish neighbour, were rent by internal dissension and dynastic quarrels, Portugal enjoyed civil peace and dynastic stability.

Conditions, men and materials for the great overseas enterprise were at hand. The inspiration behind the amazing series of voyages of discovery which began in the second decade of the fifteenth century was provided by the new dynasty, notably the Infante Dom Henrique, better known as Prince Henry the Navigator. Prince Henry was half English, the fifth of João's brilliant children, whom the poet Camões described as the *ínclita geração*, the illustrious generation, by Philippa of Lancaster, daughter of John of Gaunt. The marriage, in 1387, was the outcome of the Treaty of Windsor the previous year, the basis of the Anglo-Portuguese alliance, England's oldest continental entente.

Prince Henry, an enigmatic, ascetic figure whose motivations have given rise to endless controversy, has been variously represented as a religious fanatic, an ardent seeker after scientific truth, a ruthless materialist. He is certainly, and deservedly, a hero figure in Portuguese history. The chronicler Gomes Eanes de Azurara, writing in 1450, attributed five motives to the Atlantic voyages inspired by Prince Henry: to explore the African coast below Cape Bojador because 'neither by writings, nor by the memory of man, was the nature of the land beyond that cape known with any certainty'; to find out whether there were any Christian peoples in Africa with whom it might be possible to trade; to discover the extent of Muslim territory; to find a Christian king who might aid in fighting the Muslim; and, lastly, to extend 'the faith of Our Lord Jesus Christ and to bring to him all the souls that wish to be saved.'

A resurgence of the crusading Christian spirit of the Reconquest played an important initial part in the Portuguese overseas enterprise.

34

With the ending of the threat from Spain after Aljubarrota, the Portuguese became increasingly aggressive towards the Muslims. To do battle against the infidel was regarded as *serviço de Deus*, God's service, and in the Peninsular experience all lands were considered to have been originally Christian, the rightful patrimony of the Christians' God, which had been wrongfully usurped by the unbelievers. The successful attack on Ceuta in Morocco in 1415, in which Prince Henry took part, was the first move to carry the crusade against Islam overseas.

In Morocco the Portuguese naturally must have heard rumours of non-Muslim peoples south of the Sahara, whom they took to be Christians. Prince Henry must also have seen evidence of the Sahara gold caravans from Senegal and Upper Niger, and thus known of the existence of gold to the south. Portugal, like the rest of Europe in the last 250 years of the Middle Ages, suffered from a shortage of coin, and the search for African gold was a strong motive for Prince Henry's sending his ships southward into the Atlantic.

The voyages began soon after the Ceuta expedition, and were financed by Henry with the revenues of the Order of Christ, of which he was administrator, or with loans from the foreign banking houses and the Jewish moneylenders of Lisbon. Madeira was discovered in 1419, the Azores in 1427, but the real breakthrough came when Gil Eanes out of Lagos sailed one of Prince Henry's caravels round Cape Bojador in 1434. The Arabs called the Atlantic beyond 'the Green Sea of Darkness', and Bojador, on a waterless, harbourless coast below Morocco, was literally regarded as the edge of the world. In 1442 Antão Gonçalves·brought back the first slaves and gold dust from the coast below Bojador, evidence that Prince Henry's conjectures had been correct; in 1445 the Portuguese had reached Senegambia, where they bartered glass beads and textiles for gold, ivory and slaves, and by the mid-fifteenth century the voyages were beginning to show a profit for their promoters.

Prince Henry died in 1460, heavily in debt; but the Portuguese had already succeeded in diverting the Guinea gold trade from the Sahara camel caravans to the trading posts, *feitorias*, which they set up on the coasts. In 1457 the Lisbon mint struck the first gold *cruzado*, a coin of high purity: Portugal was on the European currency map.

But by the time of his death, Henry's vision already extended beyond Guinea gold. The fall of Constantinople to the Turks in 1453 provided an even stronger incentive to circumvent the Muslim world. A series of Papal bulls promulgated between 1452 and 1456 at Henry's instigation show that he was already intending to circumnavigate Africa and reach the Indies. Their wording was significantly illustrative of the spirit of Portuguese colonial enterprise: commending them for their apostolic zeal in winning new lands and souls for Christ, the Pope in return recognized Portugal's right to the monopoly of discovery, conquest and commerce in these areas.

Henry's rôle as instigator of overseas expansion was continued by his great-nephew João II, whose father Afonso V neglected voyages of exploration in favour of crusading excursions into Morocco and disastrous dynastic ventures in Castile. João II, one of the most remarkable of the Aviz kings, was obsessed by the idea of Prester John, the fabulously rich Christian ruler, whose domains were rumoured to lie behind the Muslim lands. Emissaries were sent in search of this legendary figure, one of whom, Pero de Covilhã, actually reached the Christian Coptic kingdom of Ethiopia in 1491, but was never allowed to leave.

Like his great-uncle Prince Henry, João II was intent on reaching the Indies; some time during the 1480's he conceived the plan of tapping the lucrative spice trade at its source in the Indian Ocean, and diverting the precious flow to Lisbon, in much the same way as Prince Henry had captured the Guinea gold trade. By 1485, a speech made by the Portuguese envoy to the Pope clearly showed his master to be already convinced that the opening of the sea route to the Indies was a possibility in the near future; three years later Bartolomeu Dias rounded the Cape of Good Hope. Subsequently the death of Prince Afonso, the heir to the throne, paralysed the king's will, whilst the implications of Columbus's voyage involved him in a series of complicated negotiations, designed to protect Portuguese interests and assert the doctrine of *mare clausum*, which culminated in the Treaty of Tordesillas in 1494. Vasco da Gama's great voyage was, however, already projected, and in 1498, early in the reign of João's successor Manuel I, da Gama sailed round the Cape and landed at Calicut on the coast of India. The way to the East was open.

When da Gama's crew disembarked, two Spanish-speaking Tunisians in the crowd awaiting them asked one man why they had come. He answered, 'We have come to seek Christians and spices.' His reply illustrates the synthesis of spiritual and material factors which

36

lay behind the Portuguese overseas enterprise, the same dual motivation which had inspired the Christian reconquest of Portuguese territory. Profit and piety were not considered to be mutually exclusive; the service of God could be combined with the service of Mammon, and the missionary followed the soldier.

The great masterpiece of fifteenth-century Portuguese art, the *Panels of St Vincent* by Nuno Gonçalves, illustrates the human background to the Discoveries. The panels, probably commissioned by King Afonso V in thanks for his Moroccan victories, depict monks, merchants, fishermen, soldiers, churchmen, even the Jewish bankers who financed the voyages, surrounding the stern black-robed figure of Prince Henry and his zealous young nephew King Afonso kneeling at the saint's feet. They are ordinary men in everyday clothes, yet for all the practicality of their expressions their eyes betray a deep religious fervour, the epic quality of an entire nation dedicated to an ideal.

These are the men who, in Camões' famous phrase, journeyed *por mares nunca d'antes navegados* – through seas none had sailed before – to circumnavigate Africa and open the sea route to the East, thus giving Europe direct contact with continents and civilizations beyond the narrow confines of the Mediterranean and the North Sea which had hitherto limited men's conception of the globe. In so doing they led medieval Europe across the threshold into the modern world in an enterprise which led to riches and empire, shipwreck and disaster, for themselves and for the colonizing powers who followed in their wake.

4   The golden age of empire

'LORD OF THE CONQUEST, navigation, and commerce of Ethiopia, India, Arabia, and Persia' was the magniloquent title Manuel I assumed. His reign (1495-1521) was Portugal's Golden Age, a unique upsurge of physical and creative achievement founded on a seaborne empire which stretched round the coasts of Africa and Asia from Morocco to Macau.

Within just over fifteen years of da Gama's landing at Calicut, the Portuguese wrested control of the valuable spice trade in the Indian Ocean from the Muslim traders, and exercised a virtual monopoly of all seaborne commerce in the area. Under the dynamic governor Afonso de Albuquerque (1509-15), they secured three key points from which they dominated the Ocean: Ormuz at the mouth of the Persian Gulf, then one of the world's richest entrepôts, through which flowed all trade between India and Persia – pearls, bullion, carpets, Arab horses, spices – Goa, the focus of their eastern Empire, with a superb harbour on the west coast of India, and Malacca in the east, seat of the wealthiest sultanate in the Malay Peninsula and centre of the spice trade.

These three strongholds, with the addition of Macau on the Chinese mainland in 1557, with a string of fortified and unfortified trading settlements, *feitorias*, from Sofala on the East African coast to Ternate in the Moluccas, formed the Portuguese *Estado da Índia*. It was essentially a trading empire, founded on naval supremacy; the Portuguese asserted a monopoly over commerce in certain commodities, issuing shipping licences, *cartazes*, and levying customs dues. Although they could not maintain a tight monopoly east of the Malacca Straits, they succeeded in extending their commerce to China and Japan, and retained their supremacy in the maritime trade of the Indian Ocean throughout the sixteenth century.

It was a remarkable achievement by any standards: that a nation of just under one and a quarter million people on the western fringe of Europe should dominate a vast and distant ocean for one hundred years. Although the Hindu and Muslim powers round the Indian Ocean at the time of their arrival were in a state of confusion, and the Portuguese ships enjoyed technical advantages over the unarmed native trading vessels, Portuguese superiority over the sophisticated peoples with whom they had to deal was negligible compared with that of the Spanish *conquistadores* over the primitive arms of the Aztecs and Incas. One of the principal reasons for the Portuguese successes in the East, as for the Spanish in the Americas, was simply their tenacity and will to win.

The products of the mercantile empire were sold through the *Casa da Índia* in Lisbon, whence they were redistributed throughout Europe in exchange for the arms, cereals, naval stores, and manufactured goods needed for its maintenance. Pepper from Malabar and Indonesia, a Crown monopoly, was the most lucrative commodity; the other principal products included: mace and nutmeg from Banda, cloves from Ternate, Tidore and Amboina, cinnamon from Ceylon, gold, silks and porcelain from China, horses and carpets from Persia and Arabia, pearls from Ormuz, cottons from Cambay and Coromandel, silver bullion from Japan, the gold of Guinea in West Africa and Monomatapa in the East, sugar from the Atlantic islands of Madeira and São Tomé, and later, towards the end of the century, from Brazil.

During the first half of the sixteenth century Portuguese attention was almost wholly concentrated on the empire in the East. Brazil, first discovered by Pedro Alvares de Cabral in 1500, was largely neglected until the 1530's, when fear of French infiltration prompted João III to plan systematic colonization of the territory. By the middle of the century, however, the diminishing returns and economic strains of the eastern empire, compared with the potentialities of Brazil, began a shift in the colonial centre of gravity from the Indian to the Atlantic Ocean. The demands of the burgeoning Brazilian sugar industry gave rise to another profitable source of income – the supply of slaves from Angola and the kingdom of the Congo to work the plantations. The rapid expansion of the industry during the last quarter of the century led planters to boast that the sugar of Brazil was worth more to the Portuguese Crown than all the spices and jewels from 'Golden Goa'.

The wealth of the Crown in the reigns of Manuel and his successor João III (1521-57) favoured an unequalled flowering in architecture and the arts. Writers, painters, and architects flocked to the Portuguese court where the cultural renaissance was directly financed and inspired by the national experience in the East.

In architecture, Oriental influences and fantasies based on the maritime adventure interacted with contemporary European traditions to produce a uniquely Portuguese style called the Manueline. While it was basically a flamboyant Gothic, with influences from the Spanish Plateresque and Moorish architecture, the Manueline acquired its individual native character through its interpretation of the symbols of the Age of the Discoveries and has been called an epic of the sea in stone.

Its first great exponent, Jean Boytac (active c. 1490-1525), was not a Portuguese but a Frenchman, probably from Languedoc. His style, an early classic Manueline, was characterized by a combination of plain surfaces with decorative detail of a Moorish delicacy and elaborateness, and his greatest achievements, the cloisters at Belém and Batalha, are among the most beautiful monuments of the period. Both Boytac and the Spaniard Juan de Castillo (active 1505 until after 1535) who succeeded him at Batalha and Belém, employed as decorative motifs the images of the early voyages: ropes, astrolabes, and the Cross of the Order of Christ which the Portuguese vessels carried on their sails. But the fascination of the Portuguese with their overseas experience was most directly conveyed in the work of the brothers Diogo (1510-47) and Francisco (1508-31) de Arruda, who developed an exuberantly naturalistic native style. In Diogo de Arruda's famous Chapter House window at Tomar, branches of coral and dripping wreaths of seaweed intertwine with ropes, buckles and sails in a navigator's vision of the tropic oceans, while the melon domes of his brother Francisco's Tower of Belém evoke the Moroccan crusades.

Renaissance influences entered Portuguese architecture first through Juan de Castillo's use of their decorative motifs, but principally in the pure Roman style of his compatriot, Diogo de Torralva (1500-66), Francisco de Arruda's son-in-law. Renaissance sculpture came to Portugal via France with the sculptors Nicholas Chanterene (active c. 1516-50) and Jean de Rouen (active c. 1530-80), successively employed by the Portuguese court. Chanterene first worked for Manuel on the Gothic west portal at Belém, but as his style developed he abandoned the Gothic for Renaissance forms and, through his work at Lisbon, Coimbra and Évora, transformed and dominated Portuguese sculpture in the sixteenth century.

Painting during the Golden Age remained deeply influenced by Flemish traditions which had permeated Portugal through close dynastic and commercial links with Burgundy in the previous century. There were three main schools: the Northern at Viseu, where the most gifted artist of the age, Vasco Fernandes, called 'Grão (Great) Vasco', lived and worked; Lisbon, where Jorge Afonso, royal painter to Manuel, counted Cristovão de Figueiredo, Garcia Fernandes and Gregório Lopes among his pupils; and Évora, centre of an artistic renaissance under its cultivated archbishops, where Frei Carlos, a Fleming and professed monk at the monastery of Espinheiro, was the principal painter. Their work, though lacking the powerful impact of Nuno Gonçalves', was vigorous, richly coloured and deeply felt, but by the middle of the century when Italian influences began to appear, Portuguese painting was already in decline.

Portuguese graphic talent was best displayed in the richly illuminated volumes of Manuel's Leitura Nova, and above all in the superb charts and atlases which were their great contribution to the technical knowledge of the Renaissance. Of the several gifted cartographers which the century produced, the most outstanding was Fernão Vaz Dourado, son of a fidalgo and an Indian woman, who lived most of his life at Goa; his beautifully executed atlases are among the masterpieces of the period. Symbolic of the age of adventure through which the country was passing, the Belém Monstrance, a masterpiece of the goldsmith's art, was wrought from gold brought back by Vasco da Gama from Kilwa in East Africa, and was the work of Gil Vicente, the great poet-dramatist of the period.

The sixteenth century was Portugal's Golden Age of literature. In poetry the work of Gil Vicente (active c. 1510-36) and above all of Luís de Camões, the genius of Portuguese verse, spanned the century. Vicente wrote in Castilian and Portuguese, and his verse plays are descriptions of contemporary manners, with the earthy popular humour, simple piety and strong lyrical feeling for nature which are the dominant traditions of Portuguese literature. The same love for and appreciation of the countryside is strong in the lyrics and eclogues of the Renaissance poets Bernardim Ribeiro and Sá de Miranda.

Lyricism is the forte of Portuguese poetry, and the poetic genius of the age, Luís de Camões, although best known outside Portugal as the author of an epic, the *Lusiads*, was also her greatest lyric poet. An innovator imbued with the spirit of the Renaissance, he recreated the language in his sonnets. Gil Vicente wrote his first plays under Manuel I, Camões died in the reign of Sebastião, his great-grandson, penultimate king of the Aviz dynasty; and nothing could illustrate more clearly the rapid cultural development of Portugal in the sixteenth century than a comparison of the direct vernacular of Gil Vicente with the sophisticated rhythm and musicality of Camões' verse.

His epic poem, the *Lusiads*, is an account of the historical exploits of the Portuguese and the voyage of Vasco da Gama. Camões himself typified his age; leaving his 'life scattered in pieces across the world', he fought in Morocco and lost an eye at Ceuta, then, exiled from the court, he wandered through the East, lived in Mozambique, Goa, Macau, sailed the Red and China Seas, and was shipwrecked in the Mekong delta with his Indo-Chinese mistress and the manuscript of the *Lusiads*. Returning to Lisbon towards the end of his life, he published the *Lusiads* in 1572, received a meagre pension from the king, and died in poverty in 1579.

While the exploits of the Portuguese overseas inspired Camões' epic poem, they also gave rise to a volume of great prose literature. The *Histories* of João de Barros and Diogo de Couto, the *Lendas da Índia* of Gaspar Corrêa, the *Peregrinação* of Fernão Mendes Pinto, and the *Tragic History of the Sea*, are amazing accounts, some at first hand, of the adventures of contemporary soldiers, sailors and traders, fighting, bartering, praying and often dying, on the coasts of Africa and Asia.

HUMANISM AND THE COUNTER-REFORMATION

João III was a cultivated man, an educational reformer and the protector of humanists and men of letters. Unfortunately for the subsequent intellectual history of Portugal he was also deeply pious and a fervent supporter of the Counter-Reformation, responsible for the introduction of the Inquisition into the country. Humanism and the Counter-Reformation in the Peninsula proved to be mutually irreconcilable.

The humanist movement in sixteenth-century Portugal began with Portuguese graduates of Italian universities at the end of the previous century. The low level of higher education made it a tradition for students to attend foreign universities: Padua, Bologna, Florence, Louvain, Salamanca, and above all Paris, the school for Portuguese humanists. In the middle years of João III's reign the future for humanism looked promising. In 1537, at the king's direction, the University, which had been at Lisbon, was transferred to Coimbra and staffed with professors from abroad; five years later the humanist André de Gouveia came from Guyenne to direct the College of Arts and recruited Portuguese from Bordeaux, Diogo de Teivo and João da Costa, with a Scot, Buchanan, as teachers, while in 1545, the best known of Portuguese humanists, Damião de Gois, a companion of Erasmus, returned to Portugal at the king's invitation, as keeper of the royal archives. However, during the same period, João III established the Inquisition in Portugal and hopes for a humanistic future in intellectual life were soon dashed. Barely a year after his return, Damião de Gois was denounced to the Inquisition for heterodoxy, while at Coimbra his fellow humanists were arrested and threatened with prosecution; the College of Arts was closed and its direction later given over to the Jesuits.

The Jesuits and the Inquisition were the twin forces of the Counter-Reformation in Portugal. Both became immensely powerful, in practice autonomous, and eventually violently jealous of each other's influence. The peculiarly totalitarian character of the Inquisition, 'the principal motor of our non-Europeanism' as one historian has called it, cut the Iberian Peninsula off from the rest of Europe behind an Iron Curtain of religious orthodoxy through which, until the mid-eighteenth century, the forces of rationalism and the Enlightenment failed to penetrate.

The powers of the Inquisition, or Holy Office as it was called, reached into every corner of Portuguese life. The office of Inquisitor General was the most prestigious and powerful in the land after the king; he commanded a horde of functionaries or familiars, and his jurisdiction was supreme over all other civil authorities. The Inquisition's strength lay in its equation of religious orthodoxy with the security of the state, and literary censorship was consequently

43

an important part of its work. But its functions extended beyond the mere pursuit of unorthodox opinion to witchcraft, abuse of the confessional and sexual aberrations.

Most of its cases, however, concerned the persecution of Judaism, which in the Iberian context was as much a social as a religious problem. Until the reign of João III, the Portuguese kings had treated the Jewish minority with relative tolerance. Although subject to heavy taxation and social discrimination, the Jews were appreciated by the sovereigns for their skills, notably as physicians and financiers, and when Ferdinand and Isabella expelled the Jews from Spain in 1492, João II allowed them to settle in Portugal. Although Manuel I, to please his mother-in-law Isabella the Catholic, threatened all Jews and Moors with expulsion or conversion in 1496, he still regarded them as useful members of the community, and executed a number of questionable manœuvres to prevent those who wanted to leave from doing so. He even issued a decree the following year which forbade inquiry into the faith of the recently – forcibly – converted.

The situation changed drastically in the reign of João III. The Inquisition regarded the 'New Christians', as the converted Jews were called, as a potential fifth column. They were persecuted as a powerful social minority on the grounds of heredity as much as religious opinions, and the Inquisition controlled the paths to advancement by the issuing of certificates of *limpeza de sangue*. These documents, which proved the bearer to be free from any taint of Jewish blood, were required for all official appointments. Jewish victims of the Inquisition included António José da Silva, the Brazilian playwright who was garrotted and burnt in 1739, and Duarte da Silva, the richest banker in Lisbon in the mid-seventeenth century, whom even the king's protection failed to save from imprisonment and exile. This sustained and ferocious persecution of the most intelligent and enterprising elements in the community was to have damaging long-term effects on Portuguese intellectual and economic life.

ECONOMIC AND SOCIAL EFFECTS OF EMPIRE
The immediate effect of the Golden Age of Empire at its outset was vastly to increase the wealth and consequently the political power of the Crown. The monarchy became inevitably more autocratic; there were only four *cortes* during the reign of Manuel

and a mere three under João III in a period of thirty years. Manuel inherited a strong royal power from João II, and greatly reinforced it by centralizing the administration, examining, revoking and reforming the privileges and donations granted to the nobility, and the charters, *forais*, of the municipalities.

The privileged classes, the nobility, the Church and the religious orders, also benefited from the economic opportunities offered by the overseas empire. The nobility became increasingly dependent on the king as the source of all wealth and privilege, but in return there were lucrative appointments to be had overseas, rich governorships and captaincies, and the chance to participate in profitable commercial enterprises. The clergy and the religious orders became deeply involved with the economics of empire. The Jesuits in particular took part in the rich trade with Japan – where their proselytizing resulted in the expulsion of the Portuguese in 1634 – and owned vast plantations in Brazil, where they did great service in educating the Amerindians and protecting them from the cruelties and oppression of the colonists.

Large-scale overseas ventures such as the equipping of the Brazil and India fleets, the exploitation of vast tracts of territory in Brazil and the slave and sugar trade in the Atlantic, required sophisticated financing and considerable capital. While at first the Crown relied heavily on foreign merchant bankers, the Italians, Germans, Flemings and Spaniards, for loans to meet the costs of empire, by the second half of the century their place was being taken by native Portuguese, the 'New Christian' financial dynasties of Lisbon, which were later to be persecuted almost out of existence by the fanaticism of the Inquisition.

Yet, however much individual classes of society may have benefited, by the middle of the century the strains of empire were beginning to be generally felt. The maintenance and defence of a chain of forts stretching from Sofala on the east coast of Africa to the Moluccas and Macau on the edge of the Pacific, strongholds in Morocco, forts and *feitorias* on the west coast of Africa, and settlements in Brazil on the other side of the Atlantic, made demands on metropolitan Portugal in terms of money, manpower and physical resources which could not possibly be met.

For the Crown at least, which bore the brunt of the expenditure, the eastern empire became a case of diminishing returns in money terms. Wealth was diverted by smuggling and embezzlement even before it reached Lisbon. Although many Portuguese colonial officials were dedicated men of the calibre of João de Castro and Afonso de Albuquerque, as Albuquerque wrote to Manuel in 1510, in an illuminating comment on the colonial administration: 'The people of India have rather elastic consciences, and they think they are going on a pilgrimage to Jerusalem when they steal.' When it did reach Lisbon, much of the profit found its way into the pockets of foreign merchants to pay for supplies for the maintenance of empire, and to repay loans; considerable sums then had to be spent on colonial administration and defence. Even during the Manueline golden years the income of the Crown did not always equal its expenses, and the king was frequently forced to have recourse to loans on the security of future pepper shipments, while in the reign of his successor there were several severe financial crises. Brazil, economically a far more viable proposition than the eastern empire, easier of access, with a healthier climate, and less expensive to maintain in terms of men and shipping, did not come into its own until the sugar industry began to boom in the late 1570's.

The empire drained Portugal of its resources not only in money, but in manpower. The total population of metropolitan Portugal according to the 1527 census has been estimated at not more than 1,400,000, and, although the population actually grew during the century, it has been estimated that some 2,400 people left Portugal yearly for overseas. Most of the emigrants were young, able-bodied men, many of them bound for Goa, a long sea voyage which took a high toll in lives, while those who survived the journey were lucky to live many years in the unfamiliar and unhealthy conditions in the East. Large tracts of cultivable land in the south and centre of Portugal which might have benefited from the increase in population remained undeveloped, since the emigrants from the overcrowded Minho and Lisbon areas, their heads turned by the 'fumes of India', preferred to try their fortune overseas, and only one-third of the population worked on the land, a significantly small proportion for a pre-industrial economy.

The strains of empire dissipated the social unity which Portugal had enjoyed under the Burgundian and early Aviz kings. Unfairly distributed burdens of taxation and severe price inflation accentuated social inequalities, and Portuguese society acquired the rigidly conservative hierarchical structure which it was to retain for centuries to come. An increasingly absolute monarch at its apex was supported by a privileged nobility and clergy above the mass of the population living in a state of relative misery. Aristocracy and Church were interlocked: the Church was the path of advancement for younger sons of *fidalgos*, and the highest ecclesiastical offices in the land rotated between the great families. In the Iberian Peninsula as a whole, one-third of the population, the nobility and clergy, owned ninety-five per cent of the land, which was the one sure source of wealth in the wild price inflation of the time. The privileged classes benefited from the riches of overseas trade, while enjoying exemption from the major burdens of taxation which bore on the remaining two-thirds of the nation, the urban population and an ignorant and miserable peasantry.

The great nineteenth-century liberal historian, Alexandre Herculano, wrote this epitaph on the sixteenth century: 'The glory which we acquired in this epoch was one of the greatest the world has seen, but we purchased it at the price of future disgrace, with the death of all hope, the bearing for centuries of a cup full of ills and affronts.'[1]

5 Foreign domination

THE GREAT CENTURY ENDED with the loss of Portugal's independence: in 1580 the Crown passed to Philip II of Spain and the country entered on a sixty-year period of foreign domination.

Philip inherited the throne through his mother, a daughter of Manuel I. The last two kings of the Aviz dynasty both died childless; Sebastião (1557-78) was only twenty-four when he met his death in Morocco at the battle of al-Ksar el-Kebir with the best of his nobility and army, who were either killed with him or captured and held to ransom; his elderly uncle and successor, Cardinal Henrique, survived him for a bare two years. Boasting 'I inherited it, I bought it, I conquered it,' Philip took the throne against minimal opposition. Portugal at the close of her Golden Age, in a state which Camões writing shortly before his death in 1579 described as a 'vile, exhausted wretchedness', *vil e apagada tristeza*, surrendered her independence without a fight.

Spain and Portugal had become increasingly drawn towards each other during the sixteenth century. Dynastically linked through a series of semi-incestuous marriages, the two courts shared common cultural, religious and economic interests. The Portuguese upper classes were bilingual in Portuguese and Castilian, and Portuguese students graduated at Spanish universities, notably Salamanca. The crusading force of the Counter-Reformation bound the two nations together against the heretical tendencies of Northern Europe, a unity of purpose which was reinforced by the needs of defence of their overseas empires against the northern powers.

Spanish and Portuguese frequently joined forces against the marauding colonial newcomers, the English, the French and, above all, the Dutch; while the bullion wealth of Spain's American empire drew Portugal into her economic orbit. The dearth of silver in

48

Western Europe during the period meant economic hegemony for Seville, the channel for Mexican and Peruvian bullion. Portuguese merchants were deeply involved in the Seville trade, and by the end of the century the Spanish silver *real* was her main unit of currency.

The Duke of Alva claimed that he conquered Portugal with 'Mexican silver bullets'; the way had been prepared by a large-scale suborning of the Portuguese nobility. Weakened physically and financially by the al-Ksar el-Kebir disaster two years before, the *fidalgos* welcomed Philip; the Inquisition and the Jesuits supported him, while the bulk of the population, traditionally hostile to Spain, was leaderless and without influence.

Spain and Portugal were joined in the Union of the Two Crowns, united – in theory – only in the person of the sovereign; the colonial empires were separately administered, and Portugal was governed directly from Lisbon. However the Portuguese, not unnaturally, regarded the sixty years of Spanish domination as a period of Babylonian captivity, a time of humiliation which saw the dismemberment of their once-proud eastern empire by the rising maritime powers. The Dutch, having recently won independence from Spain, used their state of war with that country to attack the Portuguese overseas possessions, attacks which in the East were followed up by the English and the local Muslim rulers.

Within fifty years, from 1600 to 1640, the Dutch destroyed Portugal's monopoly of trade in the Indian Ocean; in 1622 Ormuz was lost to the Persians assisted by the English, and in 1634 the Shogun closed the Japan trade. The Dutch blocked the bar of Goa for seven years, and took Malacca in 1641. In West Africa they captured el-Mina in 1637 and Arguim the following year; in Brazil they attacked and occupied territory in the Maranhão. Thus by 1640 Portugal had lost two of the three historical pillars of her maritime empire in the East, Ormuz and Malacca, their trade with Japan, and the gold of Guinea, while the Dutch menaced Angola, source of slaves for the Brazilian sugar industry, and attacked Brazil itself.

In Portugal frustrated nationalist feeling, social misery and bitterness at the present humiliation combined with a yearning for past glories gave rise to a Messianic myth, Sebastianism. In the popular mind Sebastião, who was believed to have survived al-Ksar el-Kebir, was identified with el *Rei Encuberto*, the Hidden One, a redeemer-king who would lead the nation to establish an empire of right and justice.

The psychological need for a Messiah, coupled with the belief in the workings of the supernatural common to the time, gave the myth a wide currency, even among the educated classes, up to 1640. Sebastianism as a popular phenomenon in the sixteenth and seventeenth centuries did not long survive the Restoration, but as a nostalgia, *saudosismo*, for a heroic past, and a *cri de cœur* against the frustration of contemporary conditions, it has represented a continuing theme in Portuguese literature and politics.

The revolt of 1640 by which Portugal regained her independence was not, however, a popular revolution; a gulf divided its aristocratic instigators from a miserable, politically apathetic population. The second and third decades of the seventeenth century were years of great social wretchedness, with sporadic hunger riots against the nobles and the administration which were savagely repressed. Although the ruling classes took part in the suppression of the popular risings which they saw as threats to the social order, the 1640 rebellion was the result of an increasing divergence of economic interest between themselves and the Spanish government. While the Court was at Madrid and rarely visited Lisbon, the Portuguese nobility were deprived of the diversions, privileges and honours which they regarded as their due. More important, Spain's absorption in European problems operated to the detriment of the vital Brazil trade in which many of them were involved. Finally, the needs of imperial defence caused an escalation of fiscal demands, culminating in a five per cent tax on property which sparked off the 1640 revolt. Taking advantage of the Spanish government's preoccupation with the rising in Catalonia, a group of *fidalgos* overthrew the administration in Lisbon and declared the Duke of Bragança João IV, king of an independent Portugal.

The position of the newly independent state was an unenviable one. The Portuguese, after sixty years in Spain's shadow, emerged, in the words of the great Jesuit preacher Padre António Vieira, as 'the Kaffirs of Europe', internationally isolated and internally divided. Within a year of the Restoration, a serious conspiracy in favour of Spain implicated several of the great *fidalgos*, the Archbishop of Braga and the Grand Inquisitor, *letrados* in the royal administration and one of the richest merchants in Lisbon. The people remained firmly hostile to Spain, but the nobility, clergy and merchants were torn between loyalty to an independent Portugal and the commercial attractions of the Seville trade with its much needed silver bullion and the valuable concession for the supply of slaves to the Spanish colonies. Although the Jesuits supported the new régime, principally for reasons connected with their territories in South America, their ecclesiastical rivals, the pro-Spanish Inquisition, pursued an inimical policy, persecuting the great New Christian merchants and bankers whose financial support was vital to the defence of the new kingdom.

While the government struggled with a doubtfully loyal country and a serious economic situation at home, its international position was equally precarious. Poor and without allies, Portugal had to contend for twenty years with the Dutch overseas and the Spanish on her frontiers. In return for allies she found herself obliged to exchange the political dictatorship of Spain for commercial and diplomatic exploitation by other foreign powers. The implications of her strategic position on Spain's vulnerable Atlantic side, and the commercial advantages to be gained from participation in her Brazil trade were well recognized internationally, and France, England and Holland engaged in guerrilla warfare for diplomatic and commercial ascendancy at Lisbon.

Although the France of Louis XIV dominated the imagination and the diplomacy of contemporary Europe, the accession of his nephew to the throne of Spain threw Portugal into the arms of England. Even before this diplomatic dénouement, England had exploited her oldest ally's need in order to exact the maximum economic advantage. Cromwell's treaty of 1654 with João IV laid the foundations of English commercial hegemony in Portugal, exacting 'most favoured nation' treatment for English merchants in the Portugal trade, which they regarded as 'the very best branch of all our European commerce'. From that year on, the English 'factories' at Lisbon and Oporto flourished as privileged, autonomous bodies.[1]

The break with Spain in 1640 and the subsequent search for allies brought about a certain Europeanization in Portuguese attitudes. Portuguese diplomats travelling abroad could not but note the difference in levels of culture, science and commerce between the foreign capitals they visited and those obtaining in their own country, cut off for so long from Europe by Spain and the Counter-Reformation. Portuguese society had become introverted and isolationist, rigid in mind and attitudes; an educational background which opposed faith to rationalism combined with the strong streak of fatalism in the Portuguese character to produce a prevalent mood of inertia and resistance to change. The re-emergence of Portugal in Europe in 1640 initiated a struggle between the would-be modernizers, the *estrangeirados*, foreignized Portuguese, and the old guard, the *castiços*, conservative, aristocratic and religious. This battle between the traditionalist Counter-Reformation element and the followers of contemporary European thought became an enduring feature of Portuguese political life.

6   Absolutism and Enlightenment

THE EIGHTEENTH CENTURY in Portugal, as in the rest of Europe, was the age of absolutism. The reign of João V (1707-50), the most cultivated and intelligent of the Braganças, ushered in a second cultural and artistic renaissance founded on a new inflow of colonial wealth from the gold and diamond mines of Brazil.

The Brazil trade was the key to Portugal's economy, and colonial questions occupied much of the government's attention; João V encouraged emigration to Brazil and expanded the royal administration there. The abundance of gold drew foreigners to Lisbon, anxious to participate in the profits of the Brazil trade, and in the second and third decades of the reign Portugal enjoyed a period of economic expansion.

Culturally, the Joanine era was one of great richness; foreign architects, painters, sculptors, singers, musicians and silversmiths came to Lisbon to cater to the royal taste for magnificence. The first half of the eighteenth century was the heyday of Portuguese Baroque, dominated by the German architect Ludwig, or Ludovice, in the south and the Tuscan Nazzoni, or Nasoni, in the north; the vast palace-monastery of Mafra, the great Águas Livres aqueduct, the baroque churches of Oporto and the beautiful University Library at Coimbra all belong to this period. While the major works in architecture, painting and sculpture were executed by foreigners, native artists displayed their talent for decoration in exuberant gilded woodcarving and ceramic tiles, their craftsmanship in marble and stone, and baroque wooden sculpture.

Royal patronage extended to letters as well as to the arts. In 1722 the *Real Academia da História* was founded, where *estrangeirados* such as the royal administrator Alexandre de Gusmão advanced the claims of Corneille and Molière against the *castiços'* Castilian theatre represented by Calderón. The first foreign language grammars were published, French took precedence over Latin in the education of young *fidalgos*, and courtiers who had formerly spoken only Castilian and Portuguese now prided themselves on their fluency in French and Italian.

The entire governmental system depended on the king, its strength or weakness on the royal will and energy. At the outset of his reign João V was a determined and conscientious administrator; he attempted to reform the system to make it more centralized and efficient and to assert a firmer royal control over the colonial administration. In foreign affairs he established his policy on the bases of the Anglo-Portuguese alliance and neutrality in continental conflicts, which remained the cardinal principles of Portugal's foreign policy until the mid-1960's.

In the early 1740's, however, the king fell ill, and the last decade of his reign was one of decline. The administrative reforms which the king had begun had not been completed, and with his illness the weakness of the system became apparent. The rapid expansion necessitated by economic prosperity had overloaded outdated institutions which proved inadequate to cope with the increased demands made upon them. With the king's illness the decision-making power was paralysed, administrative delays accumulated, and governmental control loosened. The direction of government fell into the hands of the cardinals, and as the king in fear of death became increasingly devout, a clerical reaction set in. When Luís Antonio Verney, once a royal protégé whom the king had sent to Rome to produce a plan for the reform of education, finally produced his *O Verdadeiro Metodo de Estudar* in 1746, its radical ideas, which included primary schools and the education of women, were considered too advanced, and it was published clandestinely and without royal support. It was a sad end to a brilliant beginning, as Père Delaunay lamented:

> *Mais quel sombre tableau frappe ici ma paupière*
> *Le souverain lui-même évite la lumière!*
> *Ce roi, né pour goûter la paix des immortels,*
> *Est réduit à gémir à l'ombre des autels...*

54

THE POMBALINE PERIOD

João V died in 1750, and his successor José I (1750–77), an ineffectual man, left affairs of state to his Prime Minister, the Marquis of Pombal. Pombal (1699–1782), one of the most controversial and remarkable figures in Portuguese history, was a contemporary of the age of the Enlightenment, and a pupil of the great diplomat and leading *estrangeirado* of the preceding reign, Dom Luís da Cunha. The *estrangeirados* attacked the ambition of the Jesuits and their stranglehold on Portuguese education, the cruelties of the Inquisition, the rigidity of the 'Old Christians', or '*Puritanos*', who refused to intermarry with anyone suspected of a taint of New Christian blood, the multiplication of the religious orders and the ignorance of the friars and the secular clergy. Above all they deplored the failure of the government to promote agriculture and industry, which resulted in Portugal's being reduced to 'the best and most profitable colony of England'.

During the twenty-seven years he ruled Portugal, Pombal attempted to reverse the trends which had set in during the last years of the previous reign: the weakening of the state and the consequent neo-feudalism of the great nobles and the Jesuits, particularly overseas, and the impoverishment of national commerce due to smuggling and the predominance of foreign merchants. In his first decade of power he reinforced the sinews of absolute government, restricted the pretensions of the great *fidalgos*, expelled the Jesuits, and attempted to regulate the commercial situation with a campaign against bullion smuggling, and the launching of state monopoly companies to compete with, and in some cases exclude, the foreign merchants. In the second decade, the 1760's, a serious crisis in the Brazil trade forced him to make strenuous efforts to stimulate home production and create new industries in Portugal and new resources overseas.

Pombal was a pragmatist rather than a pupil of the Enlightenment; his measures were reactions to the needs of the moment. Although he abolished slavery in metropolitan Portugal, expelled the Jesuits and transferred the power of censorship from the Inquisition to the *Real Mesa da Censura*, an edict of 1770 stigmatized the works of the *philosophes* as 'abominable productions of incredulity and libertinage', and banned all books by Rousseau, Spinoza, Hobbes and Voltaire. Yet although he inspired the hardest and most ruthless government Portugal had known, including acts of barbaric and unnecessary cruelty, within the historical context of Portugal at the time, Pombal had the greatness of a head of government who understood and confronted some of the problems of his country.

Although many of his commercial initiatives were destined to be short-lived, his greatest and most lasting achievements were in the field of educational reform. He shared the interest generated by Verney's O *Verdadeiro Metodo de Estudar*, and agreed with the *estrangeirados* in attributing Portugal's cultural deficiencies to the rigidity of Jesuit educational methods. He therefore aimed at the secularization of education, founded a School of Commerce and a Royal College of Nobles under the direction of the *Real Mesa da Censura*, withdrew the right to teach from the Jesuits and transferred it to lay professors paid by the state in the provincial towns. In 1772 he undertook the reform of the curriculum of the University of Coimbra, unchanged since the reign of João III 250 years before, and untouched by any new currents of thought since the Renaissance.

Pombal's reform of the University of Coimbra marked the beginning of a new epoch in Portuguese cultural history. For the first time the study of law was permitted in the light of modern thought, with Reason as the basis of the law of Nature; the natural and exact sciences were studied, and pedagogic methods brought up to date. Pombal parted the Counter-Reformation curtain between Portugal and Europe, and at last there was a place where contemporary thought could be taught and analysed.

Pombal fell in disgrace on the death of his patron José I in 1777. The reign of Maria I ushered in a wave of clerical and *castiço* reaction, later reinforced by the events in France. The chief of police, Pina Manique, instituted a reign of terror chiefly directed against intellectuals and writers like the poet Bocage who propagated the ideas of the Revolution. Nonetheless, the French cultural influences implanted by the *estrangeirados* filtered down to a nascent *petite bourgeoisie*, and a new generation educated at the reformed University of Coimbra. In 1807 the Napoleonic eagles under Junot entered Portugal and the Court fled to Brazil. The *ancien régime* was in crisis.

1 The aqueduct at Elvas – a monument of the Roman occupation.

2 Roman mosaic pavement at Conimbriga.

3 The bluff, curving prow of the traditional Tagus *fragata* (*above*) echoes the lines of the old caravels.

4 *Right:* This Hispano-Moorish earthenware bowl, dating from the first half of the fifteenth century, shows a caravel displaying the arms of Portugal on the sail.

5 The tomb of João I, founder of the Aviz Dynasty, and his English wife Philippa of Lancaster, daughter of John of Gaunt. Their marriage in 1387 sealed the alliance between England and Portugal, which still stands today.

6 One of the *Panels of St Vincent*, the fifteenth-century masterpiece by Nuno Gonçalves, shows the young King Afonso V kneeling before the saint. The black-robed man on the saint's left is the king's uncle, Prince Henry the Navigator.

7 Luís de Camões, Portugal's greatest poet, was also a soldier, a wanderer and an adventurer. He lost an eye in the Moroccan wars.

8 *Below:* Maps, charts and atlases were among Portugal's finest contributions to the growth of knowledge in the Renaissance. This map by Sebastião Lopes, dated 1558, is surprisingly close to the truth in its outlines, even if hazy on such details as the course of the Amazon.

9 *Right:* On this sixteenth-century screen a Japanese artist, with the conventional disregard for perspective, shows the arrival of Portuguese traders and Jesuit priests. This 'window to the west' remained open only briefly, and was closed again, by decree of the Shogun, in 1634.

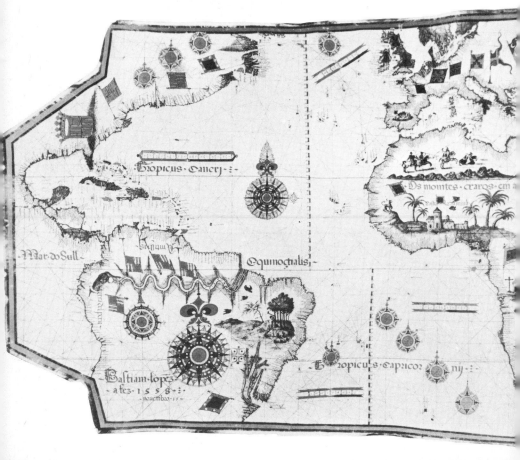

10 *Above:* Afonso de Albuquerque, Viceroy of India and a towering figure in the history of Portugal's eastern empire.

11 Vasco da Gama, leader of the historic first sea passage to India in 1498.

12 *Left:* Diogo de Arruda's Chapter House window at Tomar: branches of coral, wreaths of seaweed, ropes, buckles and sail as exuberant symbols of navigation and discovery.

13, 14 Two masterpieces of Manueline architecture, that uniquely Portuguese flamboyant Gothic: *below*, the Tower of Belém; *opposite*, the cloisters of Batalha.

15 The great Lisbon earthquake of 1755: detail of a
painting by João Glama.
On the 1st of November
the city was reduced to
ruins in a matter of sec-
onds; between 10,000 and
20,000 people were killed.

16 The Marquis of Pom-
bal, prime minister under
José I, was in effect sole
ruler of Portugal from
1750 to 1777. This portrait
shows him with plans for
the rebuilding of Lisbon
after the earthquake.

7   The liberal era

THE CRISIS OF THE OLD ORDER was long-drawn-out; it began with the flight of the Court in 1807 and ended only with the triumph of the liberal middle class in 1834.

At the dawn of the nineteenth century Portuguese absolutism appeared outwardly unchanged; established in the possession of an immensely rich Brazilian colony which largely supported the home kingdom, it headed a social structure characterized by the predominance of the aristocracy and the Church, founded on the mass of the rural population living in a state of misery and ignorance. Although the wealth of the Brazil trade had produced a perceptible increase in the numbers of the *petite bourgeoisie* in the latter half of the eighteenth century, this had in no way modified the traditional pattern of society.

At the end of the eighteenth century the middle classes, who were to emerge triumphant some thirty years later, were insignificant in numbers and influence. Out of a population of three million only 210,000 were engaged in trades or professions, concentrated in Lisbon and Oporto. The natural desire of the small middle class to improve their social position brought them up against deeply entrenched, immobile forces far more powerful than themselves. Only through a series of extraordinary events such as the Napoleonic invasions and the fierce Civil War of 1832–34 were they to succeed in overturning the social order and modifying it in accordance with their own ideals and interests.

Freemasonry, introduced by the foreign merchants, with the democratic ideals of the Revolution, had spread among a small section of the educated middle class at the dawn of the century, strengthened by the presence of the French armies. But when the Peninsular War ended, Portugal was governed by the English

Marshal Lord Beresford, and naturally inimical to revolutionary ideas. Freemasons, jacobins and liberals were persecuted, and many of them fled to Paris or to London. From exile they indoctrinated their countrymen through a series of liberal journals stressing Portugal's humiliating situation, virtually governed by the English and reduced to the status of a colony of Brazil where the royal family still lingered.

The first successful liberal revolt in 1820 was instigated by a group of middle-class professional men in Oporto, the *Sinédrio*, magistrates, doctors, lawyers and merchants, in collaboration with key local military commanders. The officers' participation in the 1820 revolt set the pattern for all subsequent coups in Portugal; the comparative weakness of the political class (which was non-existent in 1820) and the total apathy of the bulk of the population meant that no movement could hope to succeed without the support of the military. The revolutionaries of 1820 overthrew the government of Beresford, drew up a constitution, and called for the return of the King, transformed into a constitutional monarch.

The Constitution which João VI swore to uphold in 1822 laid the foundations of the constitutional monarchy during the liberal period; but the experiment of 1820 was short-lived, its complexion too democratic for the times. Within a year, a reactionary coup overturned the Constitution, which was replaced by the Constitutional Charter of 1826. On João VI's death in that year, his granddaughter Maria da Glória, daughter of his eldest son Dom Pedro, first Emperor of Brazil, was declared Queen, but two years later her reactionary uncle, the absolutist Dom Miguel, usurped the throne. A wave of repression and persecution of liberals and constitutionalists followed, culminating in civil war. Dom Pedro landed at Oporto with a force of liberal exiles and international volunteers, and the two-year War of the Two Brothers (1832-34) represented the final throes of the *ancien régime*.

The victory of Dom Pedro ensured the triumph of liberalism and of its middle-class supporters. Most of the old nobility, the clergy and the peasants (whom no one had considered hitherto, nor would consider in the future), had sided with Dom Miguel. The Civil War and, above all, the secession of Brazil in 1822 after more than a century as the focus of the Portuguese economy, severed Portugal's connection with her old way of life. After four hundred years of living off the fat of her colonial empire, the country was once again dependent on the work of her metropolitan population for subsistence and survival. With the old order in ruins, the liberal government set about creating a new one to take its place. The radical legislation of Mouzinho da Silveira, Minister of the Treasury and of Justice from 1832 to 1833, laid the foundations of modern Portugal.

The most dramatic of his measures suppressed the religious orders, confiscated their property, and revoked the donations of Crown lands. However, the result of this daring assault on the traditional structure of landholding was not, as Mouzinho hàd hoped, to effect a far-reaching land reform and enrich the state. His revolutionary legislation was employed to effect a massive transference of rural property from the religious orders and the defeated Miguelites to the supporters of the new régime. Land to the value of 50,000 to 60,000 contos,* which would have represented an invaluable source of wealth against the public debt, was sold off to create a new class of capitalist rural proprietors with a vested interest in the régime, and to confer the social status of landownership on the aspiring bourgeoisie. Describing the rapacity of the new barons, Almeida Garrett wrote: 'the baron bit the friar, devoured him, then skinned us as well...'

Disgusted by the turn of events, Mouzinho resigned and retired from public life. The Septembrist coup of 1836 led by Passos Manuel was the last throw by the extreme democratic liberals, supporters of the 1822 Constitution. The Septembrist government enacted the second great body of reforming legislation of the liberal era including the abolition of the slave trade, reform of the penal code and of primary and university education. Significantly, these radical reforms, like those of Mouzinho da Silveira, were decreed without the consent of the Cortes, which was largely composed of the more right-wing liberal supporters. When the Cortes did assemble the following year, they disputed the legislation and Passos Manuel resigned.

By 1850 the alarums and excursions of the early idealist period were over, and the middle and upper classes settled themselves firmly in the comfortable seats of power. The barons and financiers grouped under the liberal banner, while tendering a respectful nod to the slogan of 'regeneration', interpreted this as 'material betterment' in a manner calculated to favour the interests of their class. Neither of the two major parties, the *Regeneradores* and the

* One conto is 1,000 escudos.

Históricos, who succeeded each other in power from 1851, had any clear political platform, nor were they politically distinguishable from each other, save as groups of individuals round one chief or another.

Apart from the important Civil Code of 1867 and the abolition of the death penalty, government action during the period was primarily concerned with the fostering of capitalism in the development of communications, particularly railways, the foundation of banks and credit institutions, and presiding over a scene of free financial speculation. The consequences of these policies were to have far-reaching effects on Portuguese politics at the end of the century, but in the meantime the liberal constitutionalists lived peacefully in the enjoyment of power. From 1876 onwards the two parties (the *Históricos* had merged with a new group, the *Progressistas*, meanwhile) ruled by turns under the rotativist system. This negation of parliamentary government functioned in an atmosphere of increasing scandal, corruption and political cynicism until the eve of the Republic.

THE LIBERAL INTELLECTUALS

Yet for all its faults, the liberal era produced a number of major intellectuals, writers and poets who were actively committed to the fate of their country. Almeida Garrett (1799-1854), the creator of the modern theatre and protagonist of the Romantic movement, and Alexandre Herculano (1810-77), historian, polemicist, and novelist, the most influential intellectual figure of the century, both fought for Dom Pedro at the siege of Oporto. Both saw the liberal goal as the 'regeneration' of Portugal, and aimed to synthesize traditional values with modernization. They were convinced that the country's decadence could be ascribed to the absolutist system and the Church which had supported it; hence the strong anti-clerical strain in Portuguese liberalism. Influenced by the ideas of Proudhon, they believed in a constitutional monarchy which would dispense social justice as representing a return to the pre-absolutist virtues of Portuguese society.

Herculano expressed his contemporaries' hopes for their country when he wrote: 'What are we today? A nation that seeks to regenerate itself, that is being reborn. Reborn because it is pulling itself together, because it is turning in the rut in which it was tranquilly slumbering, because it is irritated by its decadence, and no longer smiles unashamed at the insults of strangers; because it is at last beginning to recognize that work is not dishonourable...' [1] This theme of regeneration rather than revolution, the restoration of a spirit destroyed by a period of misgovernment and the revitalization of the country through modern methods combined with traditional virtues, became the enduring theme of Portuguese political ideology, from the first Liberal revolt of 1820, through Republicanism to the New State of Dr Salazar.

Herculano believed in the right to work, access to property, and the raising of the educational level as necessary conditions of the liberty of the individual, the keystone of his political creed. He defended the right of the hungry, jobless peasantry to emigrate, and his books on emigration and public education were classics. He wrote a monumental *History of Portugal* in which he attacked the rôle of the Church in contributing to Portugal's decadence, and a *History of the Inquisition*. A fervent advocate of political morality, he retired from public life in 1867, disgusted with the increasing materialism, greed and corruption of politics. In this he followed the example of the two great innovators of Portuguese liberalism, Mouzinho da Silveira and Passos Manuel, political idealists who preferred to maintain their principles at all costs rather than compromise with the system.

Influential even in retirement, Herculano, leader of the first generation of liberal intellectuals, was the father figure of the second, which included writers and poets like the socialist historian Oliveira Martins, the poet Antero de Quental, and the novelist Eça de Queirós. Born in the forties and educated in the favourable climate of the liberal era, they were disturbed by the social order liberalism had created, impatient with the progress so far achieved and more conscious of the claims of social justice. Where the early liberals had been concerned with the overthrow of absolutism and the evolution of a constitutional monarchy, the 'generation of '70', as they were known, aimed to make the system more democratic. Socialism and 'Iberianism'[2] were the themes of the movement, inspired by the Paris Commune of 1871 and the brief implantation of the Spanish Republic in 1873. The period of the 1870's was one of hope and idealism for the younger generation of intellectuals; aware of the faults of the liberal bourgeois society, they still believed that it could be improved and turned in the direction of social democracy. But by the 1880's disillusionment had set in, and men like Eça de Queirós and the political satirist Ramalho Ortigão called themselves the *Vencidos da Vida*, the Defeated Ones. It was a period of polarization in Portuguese liberalism, when a gulf began to open between the supporters of constitutional monarchy and those who began to see republicanism as the only honourable solution to Portugal's problems.

THE GROWTH OF REPUBLICANISM, 1890–1910
Republican feeling was born as a reaction against the ossification of ideology and politics in the late nineteenth century; all projects of reform broke against the régime's fear of innovation and its supporters' interest in maintaining the status quo. Republicanism as an extreme left-wing current of liberal thought had made fleeting appearances on the fringes of politics during the century, but at least until the 1870's it had been confined to a small group of intellectuals and totally without influence. However, the growth of capitalism and the development of communications after 1850 wrought significant changes in Portuguese social and political life during the last quarter of the nineteenth century. From 1870 to 1890 the urban population increased by 16.6 per cent, whereas previously the ratio between urban and rural population had shown no noticeable change. Industrialization and improved communications were creating a new urban working class. With the decline of the Socialist party in the 1880's, the Republican party became the only serious alternative for those dissatisfied with the status quo, but its following was still insignificant.

One event above all brought about the discredit of the constitutional monarchy and the emergence of the Republican party as a serious political force: the British Ultimatum of 1890.

The question concerned Portuguese Africa, in which there had been a strong revival of interest after the secession of Brazil. The accession of the liberal government ushered in a period of more vigorous efforts at annexation, almost doubling the area under Portuguese control by 1861. However, the expeditions of Livingstone and Stanley ended Portugal's comfortable centuries-old isolation in Africa and whetted the appetites of the European powers for colonial territories. The quarrel between England and Portugal centred on the 'Rose-coloured map', published by the Portuguese government in 1886, which showed the entire territory between

Angola on the West African coast and Mozambique on the Indian Ocean to be part of the Portuguese empire. The British government under the Marquess of Salisbury challenged this title; the explorer Serpa Pinto led an expedition up the Shiré river, and on 11 January 1890 the British minister warned the government that if their troops continued to occupy the disputed area he would leave Lisbon. The Portuguese then asked for arbitration, which Lord Salisbury refused. In the face of this ultimatum by a superior power, which was also Portugal's closest ally in the councils of Europe, the government backed down.

Shocked by the government's 'servile' reaction to the English 'insult to the historic image of the country', people flocked to join the Republican party. The Ultimatum crystallized opposition to the régime; ironically the Bragança monarchy was doomed by the action of the British government which had supported it since the Napoleonic era. In the second parliamentary session of 1890, the city of Lisbon returned three declared Republicans and one sympathizer with huge majorities in a clear popular verdict on the Ultimatum and the monarchy; and early in the following year an abortive Republican revolt broke out in Oporto. The government then began a systematic persecution of the Republican party which it had hitherto ignored, with suspension of civil rights, the use of police spies and imprisonment. The party abstained from elections in protest against the manifest electoral violence practised by the régime, and devoted its energies to a nation-wide propaganda effort.

Within twenty years of the Ultimatum the Republican party had become the most powerful and coherent political force in the country, supported by all classes (with the exception of the Church and the political élite) – rich landowners, high officers in the Army and Navy, lawyers, professors, former socialists, and the urban proletariat. Freemasonry and secret societies like the Carbonária provided its militant arm. In 1908 the Carbonária assassinated the King, Carlos I, and two years later on 5 October 1910 Portugal became a Republic.

The liberal constitutional monarchy ended in an atmosphere of political cynicism and corruption; the idealism which had brought it into being had degenerated into a blatant materialism, while the social order on which it rested had become as rigid and immobile as that of the *ancien régime* it replaced. The monarchy fell because the time was ripe for its fall; discredited, corrupt, a capitalist administration whose results were seen to be the enrichment of its servants. Regarded as the author of Portugal's international humiliation at the time of the Ultimatum, and of the frequent financial crises which led to the abandonment of the gold standard in 1892, the constitutional monarchy was made the scapegoat for the country's ills.

On the credit side, nineteenth-century liberalism had laid the foundations of modern Portugal, reformed the administration, humanized the penal code, modernized the economic life of the country, and above all, propagated secular education. It was responsible for one of the great periods in Portugal's cultural history. Improved educational opportunities, freedom of thought and expression and contact with the intellectual currents of contemporary Europe released the creative energy pent up over two centuries of stagnation and repression. Almeida Garrett and Alexandre Herculano, the novelists Eça de Queirós and Camilo Castelo Branco, the poets Antero de Quental, Guerra Junqueiro and Cesário Verde, to name but a few, represented an outpouring of literary talent unequalled since the sixteenth century.

8   The Republic 1910-26

THE REVOLUTION OF 1910 had been so long in coming that it was almost an anticlimax; it was neither violent nor, in its outward aspect, revolutionary. It simply removed the head of state in the person of the king, while leaving the institutions of the liberal state untouched.

The new Republic enjoyed widespread support among the majority of politically conscious Portuguese, and embraced a wide spectrum of opinion from high-ranking military officers and the professional classes to labour leaders and the urban proletariat. This consensus was, however, more apparent than real; the vagueness of the Republican party programme, which had been its strength before the Revolution, concealed the natural disparity of views between its supporters. Before 1910, all Republicans were united in one objective, the removal of the king, and the party political programme raised no specific issues on which any section could disagree. The themes to which the country rallied, regeneration and overseas expansion, represented complete continuity with the objectives of the old liberal régime. The opening verse of the new Republican hymn, *A Portuguesa*, offered no new Utopia, but a harking back to former imperial glories:

> *Heroes of the sea, noble people,*
> *Nation valiant and immortal,*
> *Raise today once again,*
> *The splendour of Portugal.*

The movement which transformed Portugal from a monarchy into a republic appeared, therefore, to be essentially conservative. It was only later that its revolutionary implications became apparent, shattering the unity of the original Republican party. Each section of Republican opinion had its own views of the direction the new state should take, and it was not long before the fissures in the fabric began to show.

The first provisional government represented almost all the various themes of Republican ideology, and included its leading figures. The President, Teófilo Braga, was a noted positivist and contemporary of Antero de Quental at Coimbra University; the Minister of the Interior, António José de Almeida, was a convert to Republicanism at the time of the Ultimatum; Bernardino Machado, the Minister for Foreign Affairs, had been a minister under the old liberal régime, while the Minister of Justice, Afonso Costa, was a left-wing radical.

Within six months the provisional government, in which Afonso Costa played the leading part, had demonstrated its revolutionary nature, ruthlessly demolishing – or attempting to demolish – the remaining features of the old order of which it disapproved. The Church, bulwark of the constitutional monarchy, was the prime target of its hostility. Afonso Costa believed that religion was destined to disappear, and set out to remove all official vestiges of Catholicism: religious teaching in schools and universities, and the public observance of saints' days as holidays. The Church was disestablished, parish administration handed over to lay committees and revenues restricted to the offerings of the faithful. With the traditional Church, the new Republicans attacked the aristocratic aspect of Portuguese society, the 'peers' of the previous era, the barons and viscounts of finance and politics, and the old aristocracy. Titles were abolished and careers opened to talent, fostered by the foundation of new universities at Lisbon and Oporto, providing free or virtually free education.

Moderate Republicans were shocked and alarmed by Costa's radical attacks on the Church, and the unity of the party began to dissolve. The first elected government excluded the members of the former Provisional government, but Afonso Costa's partisans seized control of the executive at the party congress in October 1911. In the following year three distinct parties were formed: the Evolutionists under António José de Almeida, Brito Camacho's Unionists, and the left-wing Democrats, headed by Afonso Costa.

While party political and ideological unity dissolved into faction and intense personal rivalry, the successive Republican governments came under attack from both right- and left-wing forces in the

74

country. An unsuccessful monarchist uprising in 1912 led the government to limit freedom of speech and impose censorship of the press; political arrests once more became common, and the prisons were filled with militant labour leaders as well as dissident monarchists. The Republican régime had legalized the right to strike, a weapon which the labour movement employed with increasing violence and excess. In 1912 there was a general strike in Lisbon and other cities; labour unrest continued throughout the Republican era and contributed largely to the eventual discredit of the régime.

The working-class section of Republican support, like the moderates, old liberals, and radicals, had its own opinions as to the aims of the Revolution and its subsequent policies. It regarded the Republic as having been made by the proletariat for the proletariat, while the political architects had aimed at a democratic but not a proletarian structure. Within the working-class movement itself, moreover, the influence of the moderate socialists succumbed to the militant forces of the anarchists and syndicalists who aimed to destroy the state. Both were involved in a revolutionary conspiracy in 1913, whose primary object was the overthrow of Afonso Costa, the most radical of all the political leaders, and in the war years, 1914-17, left-wing figures were even implicated in attempted monarchist coups.

Intense party faction resulted in extreme political instability and a bewildering series of government changes. In 1917, Sidónio Pais, the leader of a coup against Afonso Costa, attempted to reform what he saw as the endemic weakness of the Republican political structure, by substituting a presidential system modelled on the United States and Brazil. He introduced universal suffrage with voting rights for illiterates for the first time, and made the presidency subject to direct election. Elected President, he dissolved parliament and governed as a dictator. In an attempt to reunite the country he made overtures to the Church, revoked several of Costa's anti-clerical measures, and reopened relations with the Vatican. However, beyond a messianic belief in himself as the saviour of his country, Sidónio Pais had no specific programme, and his régime was cut short by his assassination in December 1918. In March 1919 the Democrats regained power and the country entered on a period of even greater instability, with five Democratic governments in the course of one year.

In a broad sense Portugal shared the contemporary experience of other European countries: financial confusion, political and social instability. The success of the Bolshevik revolution in 1917, combined with price inflation and food shortages caused by the war, made the working classes increasingly militant. 1920-25 ushered in a vertiginous series of strikes with their inevitable concomitant of bloody confrontations between workers and troops. Professional revolutionaries and monarchist *agents provocateurs* stimulated working-class hostility to the government. It was a period of political thuggery and uprisings; in 1921 the Lisbon garrison mutinied, and in the same year terrorists kidnapped and assassinated the Prime Minister, Dr Granjó, and other politicians, including Machado Santos, one of the leaders of the October Revolution.

Militancy and subversion were, however, the symptoms rather than the causes of social unrest under the Republic. The root of the trouble lay in the desperate economic situation. The Republicans inherited from the monarchy a condition of chronic financial insolvency which they exacerbated with ambitious colonial schemes and, above all, by their decision to enter World War I. Portugal's abandonment of her traditional policy of neutrality in continental conflicts was a grave mistake which had the most damaging repercussions on her vulnerable economy and ultimately on the fate of the liberal Republican experiment.

The decision to enter the war stemmed largely from the government's colonial preoccupations in Africa. The Republicans were historically committed since the days of the Ultimatum to a policy of expansion and defence of the African territories, and the government feared, with justification, that German aggrandisement in Africa would be made at Portuguese expense. The Portuguese were aware of a secret Anglo-German agreement to that effect in 1898-9, and in May 1913 the two powers seemed to be on the verge of concluding another. The government realized that if Germany won the war, Portugal's African territories would be taken from her, and was therefore determined to be present at the eventual peace conference. Early in 1916, in response to the seizure of German shipping in the port of Lisbon, Germany declared war on Portugal.

The costs and consequences of the war situation on Portugal's weak economy proved unendurable. Food shortages and price inflation contributed to social unrest; by 1920 the 1910 price level had multiplied by twelve, while the wage index increased relatively by only four and a half times. The value of the escudo fell dizzily and the external debt, swollen by the costs of the Flanders expeditionary force – a bill of eighty million pounds – reached alarming proportions. Between 1919 and 1926 total deficits reached 1,500,000 contos.

Preoccupied with the worsening financial situation and involved in internecine rivalries, the Republican politicians failed to see the dangers ahead. The Portuguese bank-note scandal[1] of 1925 was symptomatic of the prevailing atmosphere of financial laxity and confusion, and of the extent to which the government had lost administrative control. There was a growing feeling that a definite solution must be found to this intolerable situation, an answer inspired by the success of Fascism in Italy and of Riverismo in Spain. In 1924 Raul Proença, a member of the Seara Nova group of liberal intellectuals which included the brilliant ex-Minister of Education, António Sergio and the historian Jaime Cortesão, warned that the opinion 'only a dictatorship will save us' could be heard on all sides. There were three unsuccessful military revolts in the course of the following year, and on 28 May 1926 a new coup began in Braga, led by General Gomes da Costa. Resistance was minimal; ten days later President Machado resigned, and on 3 June Gomes da Costa entered Lisbon. It was the end of the First Republic.

The revolution of 1926 caused almost as little civil and political upheaval as had the revolution of October 1910. The last Democratic government fell, and the liberal régime with it because it was too weak to defend itself and because, like the monarchy, it had lost the sympathy and support of the influential classes. It fell, like the monarchy, because it had failed to solve the country's chronic financial insolvency, in consequence of which Republicanism had come to be identified not with national regeneration but with continued international humiliation. With its unedifying record of political intrigue and unstable governments, the Republican régime alienated moderate opinion and the powerful business and military élite, while it failed to provide an inspiration for the young, whose idealism found an outlet in nationalism.

Many Republican party figures were men of the highest integrity and intellectual calibre, but the system which they represented had not worked, or more fairly, had not had time to work. The central tragedy of the Portuguese liberal era lay in the inherent instability of parliamentary democracy in a situation where the bulk of the electorate was illiterate or politically unconscious. The apathy of the majority, conditioned by centuries of backwardness, meant that public life could be the concern only of a minority. The absence of popular participation made democratic government in the true sense an impossibility; weakened by the lack of a power base, the parliamentary régime became a political party game of personal rivalry, faction and intrigue. While the liberal Republicans fully realized that only education could remedy the lack of a democratic tradition, they were fighting against time, and their manifest failure to provide a satisfactory answer to the country's problems meant that they were given less than two decades to prove the validity of their system.

9   Salazar and the New State

DEBT WAS THE MOST PRESSING problem facing Portugal in 1926. The budget deficit which the previous Democratic government had shown as 63,565 contos in fact totalled 330,000. Externally, the huge war debt accumulated in London loomed as an intolerable burden on the country's future. The military government negotiated the total down to twelve million pounds, but even this could not be paid, and they were forced to apply to the Finance Committee of the League of Nations, which had granted loans to the defeated countries. However, the League suggested the appointment of a commission to supervise the collection of Portuguese customs dues as the condition for a loan, and this was refused as humiliating to the national honour.

In these difficult circumstances the government, now partly military and partly civilian, invited António de Oliveira Salazar, a professor of economics at Coimbra University, to take over the Ministry of Finance. Salazar took office in April 1928, on condition that he alone should exercise full control of revenue and expenditure.

It was the beginning of forty years of personal rule, the strongest government Portugal had known since Pombal. Brilliant but cautious, conservative yet revolutionary, deeply religious and politically ruthless, Salazar was one of the most enigmatic statesmen of modern times. He came from a background of rural conservatism, born in the hamlet of Vimeiro near Santa Comba Dão in the rich wine-growing Dão valley in central Portugal, where his father was bailiff on a local estate. His mother was strongly religious and he himself was educated at the seminary in Viseu until he went to study at Coimbra University in 1910, the year of the declaration of the Republic.

At Coimbra he studied law and economics, became a professor and wrote a thesis on the gold exchange rate, and papers on the wheat problem and the control of public expenditure. His early political associations were with a Catholic group, the Academic Centre of Christian Democracy, and in 1921 he was elected Catholic deputy for Guimarães. Salazar attended only one session; he saw no virtue in parliamentary democracy outside its Anglo-Saxon context and his brief experience in 1921 only reinforced his views.

On taking office in 1928, Salazar saw two solutions to Portugal's problems: financial solvency and strong government. He was determined to cure the chronic indebtedness which had plagued the country for centuries and brought her to her present humiliating condition. His twin objectives were balancing the domestic budget and reducing the external debt, and in his first year in office he achieved a budget surplus by cutting down on expenditure and adding new taxes. A balanced budget was the keystone of his economic theory, and budget surpluses continued throughout his years in power.

Salazar's achievements in the financial sphere were remarkable. In the decade up to World War II he reduced the national debt, improved the balance of payments, built up gold and foreign exchange reserves and put Portugal back on the gold standard in 1931. His financial policies brought the country through the world economic crisis of 1929-31, and the budget surpluses he achieved were deployed to lay the foundation of future economic development. Salazar saw gradual industrialization as the means of raising the country's standard of living. Resources were invested in essential infrastructure – roads, bridges, ports, and hydro-electric schemes – which should provide the basis for a modernization of the economy and increased production.

He became prime minister, *Presidente do Conselho*, in 1932, the office which he held under successive presidents until incapacitated by a stroke in 1968. He was convinced of the need for a strong, stable government, and of a new system to replace liberal parliamentary democracy and party politics. 'Parliamentary democracy has resulted in instability and disorder, or, what is worse, it has become a despotic domination of the nation by political parties. When matters come to a climax dictatorships are created... so that a new beginning can be made', he wrote.

Salazar's 'new beginning' was the creation of his *Estado Novo*, the New State, under the Corporative Constitution of 1933. This involved a complete restructuring of the Portuguese state, and its principal effect was to transfer political power from the legislative body, the National Assembly, to the executive, under the prime minister. The prime minister himself was constitutionally responsible only to the president as head of state, and not to parliament. The *Estado Novo* was to be a corporate state; dialogue between government and governed was to be channelled through corporations identified with all major cultural, economic and religious groups and represented in a consultative Corporate Chamber.

The New State was, and is, authoritarian, hierarchical and strongly centralized. All political parties were banned, the only authorized group being Salazar's *União Nacional*, called a civic association, which supported the régime. Civilian organizations such as the *Movimento Nacional Feminino* (Women's National Movement), and the *Mocidade Portuguesa* (Portuguese Youth) were set up, with a paramilitary civil defence force, the *Legião Portuguesa* (Portuguese Legion), to supplement the ordinary police, the Republican National Guard, and the security police, the PIDE. Article 8 of the Constitution declared: 'Special laws shall govern the exercise of the freedom of expression, education, meeting and of association.' Salazar was determined to crush opposition, which he saw as destructive to the state and the nation.

On internal economic policy he was committed to free enterprise; he believed that the state should intervene to regulate the economic life of the country but without competing with private enterprise. His ideas on the relations between capital and labour were conditioned by the Catholic answer to Marxism based on the social encyclicals of Popes Leo XIII and Pius XI. Strikes and lockouts were equally forbidden under the Statute of Labour of 1933, and disputes were to be settled by collective bargaining between the state-recognized trade unions, the *sindicatos*, and the employers' associations, the *gremios*.

Under Salazar the Church regained the position it had lost in the Republican period. His early Catholic training deeply influenced his thinking, and although he believed in the separation of Church and State he saw the Catholic religion as one of the traditional strengths and virtues of the Portuguese nation. The contemporary Church had been considerably strengthened and purified by its disestablishment and by the revivifying experience of the Fátima apparitions in 1917. Salazar believed that Church and State should co-operate, and under the terms of the 1940 concordat which regulated their relations, episcopal appointments were to be submitted to the government for consideration. Significantly, in his speech on the concordat he linked the rebirth of the nation with its Catholic tradition, harking back to the Reconquest: 'We return, with all the force of a nation reborn, to the great source of our national life, and without any sacrifice of the material progress of our time, we aim to place ourselves on the same spiritual level as eight centuries ago.'

The same historical Catholic viewpoint, the spirit of the Reconquest and the Counter-Reformation, coloured his attitudes to external as well as internal questions. He regarded Marxist communism as the primary threat to western civilization, and Iberian solidarity as an essential element in the defence of that civilization. Possession of the Peninsula would represent a great strategic prize for the communist bloc, and Salazar saw the Spanish Civil War in that context, as he was later to view Portugal's war in Africa as part of the global struggle against communism. He considered the success of Franco and the nationalists in Spain as a matter of life and death for Portugal, foreseeing that a triumphant republic backed by Russia would represent a grave threat to his country. Despite British pressure he only reluctantly accepted the principle of non-intervention; his sympathies were openly with Franco.

Although disagreeing with Britain on non-intervention in the Spanish struggle, in face of the approaching war in Europe, Salazar reverted to his country's historic policy of neutrality within the framework of the Anglo-Portuguese alliance. He was fully conscious of the strategic value of Portugal's position with her Atlantic coast and islands and her ports in Mozambique on the Indian Ocean, and aware of the implications of the alliance with Britain for the defence of the whole Peninsula.

Within the alliance one of Salazar's major contributions lay in his influence with Franco. In 1939 Spain and Portugal signed the *Pacto Iberico*, a mutual non-aggression agreement, and, although Spain later adhered to the Axis anti-Comintern pact, Salazar played an important part in restraining Franco from actually joining forces with Germany. The Portuguese government acted as a link between the Allies and Spain through which aid could be sent to enable her to resist Hitler's pressure and keep out of the war; while the *Pacto Iberico* gave Spain the assurance that no attacks would be aimed at her through Portugal. Finally, at a meeting in Seville in 1942, Salazar convinced Franco that the Allies would eventually win the war, a conviction that led him later to acquiesce in the North African landings.

In the economic war, Salazar used his neutrality to extract the maximum profit for Portugal by selling wolfram to both sides until 1944. Nevertheless he kept to the spirit of the alliance, supplying Britain with escudos in return for sterling credits while other neutrals insisted on gold for their currencies. The Azores base agreement of 1943 represented a vital strategic gain to the Allies by allowing them to use the islands as anti-submarine and transatlantic refuelling bases.

10   The last years of Salazar

PORTUGAL'S POSITION in 1945 could be compared extremely favourably with the nadir she had reached after the First World War. The régime's achievements were undeniable: when Salazar came to power the country was bankrupt, internally troubled and internationally a nullity. Neutrality within the context of the Anglo-Portuguese alliance had brought her the economic benefits of neutralism with the advantage of having chosen the right side. Portugal, unlike Spain, was not isolated internationally after the war, and fitted naturally into the framework of the Atlantic alliance.

Economically the position had vastly improved; the escudo, backed by large reserves of gold and foreign exchange, stood as one of the world's hardest currencies. Internally the administration had been reorganized, roads, railways, and telecommunications extended, harbours and bridges built, and flood protection, irrigation and hydro-electric schemes carried out. The production of wheat, rice, beans and oil had been vastly increased, eliminating the need for heavy imports of these basic foodstuffs with their adverse effect on the balance of payments.

During the 1950's, industrial production began to grow at a spectacular rate, particularly in those industries which had received special stimulus under the Second Development Plan: metallurgy, chemicals, manufacturing, electrical equipment, machine tools, fertilizers, paper and pulp. In 1959 the Banco de Fomento was created as a semi-public investment bank for metropolitan Portugal and the overseas territories, designed for the granting of credit to industry, agriculture, communications and energy projects in accordance with the priorities laid down in the government's development plans. Over the period 1953-60 the annual growth rate for industrial production caught up with that of the more developed European countries and, at an average 8.1 per cent, was one of the highest in Europe, while total energy output trebled during the decade.

On the eve of the sixties, Portugal seemed to be riding towards an economic boom. In February 1957 the *Manchester Guardian*, hardly a friend of the régime, commented: 'Portugal, though pervaded by feudal manners, looks from the outside a much cleaner and neater country than when he [Salazar] took over.' And it was a much neater, cleaner, more prosperous country than the Portugal of the early twenties; living standards had risen, albeit slowly, and it had enjoyed twenty-five years of internal peace and political stability. Moreover, Salazar's careful financial policies and price controls protected the country from the inflation which hit the rest of Europe during the fifties.

It was, however, during this same decade of economic promise that internal opposition to the régime began to grow, at least among the intellectuals. For them stability had been purchased at the price of freedom of expression, economic progress at the expense of social welfare, and price stability had taken its toll of the living standards and actual wages of the rural and industrial working classes. They contrasted the excellent growth rate of industrial production with the dismal fact that Portugal's *per capita* income was the lowest in Europe. And beyond all this, with greater economic prosperity, as memories of poverty and unrest faded, came the desire for more freedom of expression, for political change, and more liberal policies.

Events began to move fast from 1958; after World War II, opposition elements coalesced in MUD (*Movimento de Unidade Democrático*), but the movement soon fragmented and the more moderate sections reformed in MND (*Movimento Nacional Democrático*). The opposition became more vocal, and the banned Communist party more active, while the administration reacted with increasing severity. From 1954 there were waves of arrests, mainly of liberal intellectuals and communists; but in 1956 a resolution laid before the *União Nacional* complained that the rich were getting richer while the standard of living of the working classes was actually declining. In 1957 the Ministry of Education dissolved the students' syndicates, and police dealt roughly with demonstrating students; in the same year virtually all opposition candidates withdrew from the elections for the National Assembly on the grounds that there was no chance of these being freely conducted.

For the 1958 presidential election all elements of the opposition focused themselves around General Humberto Delgado, the only candidate to run against the official nominee, Admiral Américo Tomás. Delgado, fifty-two years of age and eccentric, had once been a supporter of Salazar. He had no programme beyond a declared intention to dismiss the prime minister; the *New York Times* noted that, although there were real grievances, it could hardly be said that the electorate was aflame with discontent, and that many people supported Delgado only as a symbol of change. Admiral Tomás won the election by 758,998 votes to Delgado's 236,528.

The growth of internal opposition to the Salazar régime coincided with increasing hostility towards Portugal on the international scene. Although Portugal joined NATO in 1949, her original application for membership of the UN had been turned down owing to the opposition of the Soviet Union, and she was only finally admitted in 1955. Unfortunately for Portugal, the year of her admission coincided with the beginning of the anti-colonial campaign launched at the Bandung Conference, and at the UN she found herself increasingly isolated and subjected to bitter attacks on her continuing presence in the African territories of Angola, Mozambique and Guiné.

1961 was the year of crisis. Early in the New Year, following the UN Declaration on Colonialism of December 1960, Henrique Galvão, an oppositionist linked with Delgado, hijacked the luxury liner *Santa Maria* in a successful attempt to draw world attention to the situation in Angola. On 15 March armed African nationalist groups crossed the northern Angolan border from the Congo and the Angolan war began. In December of the same year India, under Pandit Nehru, annexed 'Golden Goa', which had been Portuguese since the early sixteenth century. In 1962 Delgado engineered an abortive military uprising in the garrison at Beja in the Alentejo. In 1963 guerrilla operations began in Portuguese Guinea, and in Mozambique the following year a nationalist group, FRELIMO, under Eduardo Mondlane, commenced their campaign on the northern frontier with Tanzania.

The last years of Salazar were dominated by the African question. While to the rest of the world in 1961 it appeared that Portuguese presence in Africa could not long survive, Salazar denounced the 'winds of change' as 'a meaningless phrase', and declared Portugal's determination to remain. From 1961 the nation's military, diplomatic and propaganda resources were dedicated to the maintenance of that presence. At home, the immediate effect of the war in Africa and the violent attacks on Portugal in the UN and the foreign press was to rally the nation behind Salazar. Opposition became unpatriotic; only the most dedicated oppositionists dared express the opinion that the African territories should be abandoned, for the climate of public opinion was against them. Few Portuguese believed then, and comparatively few do now, that the African provinces should be handed over to the relatively small groups of nationalist organizations.

Yet, while the nation as a whole supported Salazar's stand on Africa, by the mid-1960's there was a widespread feeling that he should retire, that the country had outgrown the period of tutelage, and that the time had come for a liberalization of the régime – politically, socially, and economically. Even the business élite who supported Salazar down the line politically were grumbling that his outmoded economic ideas were braking the progress of the country. But Salazar had no intention of retiring; convinced that no one could replace him, he carried on until a severe stroke in the autumn of 1968 ended his forty years as virtual ruler of Portugal.

Salazar died in 1970, an enigma to the end. An obituary described him as 'the volunteer of solitude'; few people knew him well, almost no one was close to him. A recluse by nature, with a fierce pride in his own integrity and incorruptibility, he lived simply in Lisbon, in a house symbolically overlooking the Palácio de São Bento, seat of the National Assembly.

Respected, hated or venerated by his countrymen, few would deny that Salazar had greatness. Through intellectual power, force of will, and an absolute single-mindedness, he dominated Portugal for forty years, revolutionizing both her economy and her political system. A high-minded patriot, he was also ruthless and cynical, true to the traditions of the Counter-Reformation Church which looked to the end, not the means. Imbued with a deep sense of his country's past, he was conscious of its future; that people should suffer in the present seemed relatively unimportant to him. Salazar's régime restored the traditional hierarchic form of Portuguese society and politics, and wiped out a century of liberal experiment, but at the same time it projected the country into the modern industrial world. The test of the validity of that system will be in its evolution.

11 Caetano's Portugal

ON THE SURFACE, Portugal in the seventies appears to be almost indistinguishable from the country ruled by Salazar. The political system is his creation; the result of the drastic remodelling of the power structure in the thirties which produced his *Estado Novo*. The vital changes which have taken place since 1968, an imperceptible shift in the balance of power, new political perspectives, and a renewal of the struggle between right and left within the regime itself, are concealed behind a structure which remains basically the same as that laid down in 1933.

Under the Constitution of 1933, Portugal is a unitary corporative republic comprising metropolitan Portugal, the Atlantic islands, and the overseas provinces. The chief of state is the president, elected by an electoral college for a seven-year term which can be repeated. The president chooses the prime minister and can dismiss him, appoints the ministers nominated by the prime minister, approves laws and decrees, and has the right of convocation and dissolution of the National Assembly. He is not answerable to the Assembly and cannot be dismissed by it. He is assisted in his constitutional functions by a consultative Council of State consisting of fifteen members. Five of them are *ex-officio* – the prime minister, the presidents of the National Assembly, the Corporate Chamber and the Supreme Court, and the attorney-general – the remaining ten are life appointments, usually ex-ministers or former presidents of the Assembly and the Chamber.

The head of the government is the prime minister, the *Presidente do Conselho*, the office formerly held by Dr Salazar. In actual executive terms the prime minister is the most powerful figure in the land, the fount of all patronage, and responsible only to the president for his actions. His ministers are responsible to him alone, and he holds in his hands all the official reins running from the apex of the power structure to its base. As prime minister he controls the country through his legislative and executive powers, through direct lines to local government – appointed civil governors of districts and presidents of municipal councils – the regime's political association, the former *União Nacional*, now the *Acção Nacional Popular*, the police forces, the National Assembly and the Corporate Chamber. The government is the permanent legislative organ of the state, and its law-making powers are more extensive than those of the parliament, the National Assembly. The government issues decree laws which have the same validity as ordinary laws, while the National Assembly votes only 'the bases of laws which the executive then elaborates.

The National Assembly, *Assembleia Nacional*, is heir to the medieval *cortes* and the parliamentary Chamber of Deputies, although its powers are considerably reduced in relation to the executive. It consists of 130 members elected by direct suffrage for the districts of metropolitan Portugal, the islands, and the overseas provinces for a four-year term and normally sits for three months of the year, from November to April. It votes the bases of the laws and authorizes the annual budget. It is the principal forum for discussion of political measures, its debates are reported in the press, and members do have the right to put forward projects for laws provided they are not related to revenue or expenditure.

The government controls the Assembly through its political organization, the *Acção Nacional Popular* (ANP). Parties are officially banned in Portugal since Salazar regarded them as the source of the country's ills under the monarchy and the republic, and the ANP is therefore termed a 'civic association'. It is, however, in effect the government party which was led by Dr Salazar for forty years and is now headed by his successor as prime minister, Professor Marcello Caetano. At general elections deputies are elected on block lists, and although at election times opposition groups are allowed to present their candidates, the ANP lists usually win.

Before the Assembly may discuss bills laid before them by the government, the measures are considered by the *Câmara Corporativa*, the Corporate Chamber. The Chamber is a purely consultative body with no legislative powers, but its opinions, *pareceres*, have considerable influence. Under the theory of the Corporate State, the Chamber is the alternative to the parliamentary system, and provides for national participation in public affairs by consultation and a direct dialogue between interest groups and the executive. It consists of 185 delegates of twelve corporations which in Salazar's theory of the corporate state cover every section of Portuguese life – agriculture, trade, fishing, local government, the civil service etc. In fact, although pre-corporative organizations have existed since 1933, the first corporations were set up in 1954 and only completed with the institution of the last three corporations in 1966. In practice the Chamber is a largely conservative body, controlled by the government which appoints a proportion of the delegates of the various corporations and the Chamber's executive officials. Its principal utility lies in the reports drawn up by the sections and subsections of the component corporations on proposed government measures which concern their particular interests.

Such are the official organs of the state and the traditional power lines bequeathed by Salazar to his successor Caetano. Outwardly things are the same, but within the structure of the state there has been a perceptible shift in the centre of gravity. In his thirty-six years as prime minister, Salazar dominated Portugal absolutely, holding all the reins in his hands, while the successive presidents of the republic were really figureheads. Since Salazar's retirement and death, however, the president, Admiral Américo Tomás, has emerged from his shadow to be seen as a figure of some stature and influence. Already in his second term in 1968, he held the balance in the critical interregnum period after Salazar's stroke, when he appointed Caetano from among the other contenders for the premiership. During that interregnum, the potential implications of his constitutional powers became apparent, and his standing was greatly enhanced. Admiral Tomás, a benevolent, paternal man, is in fact deeply conservative, and enjoys the support of the powerful right wing. The passing of Salazar underlined the fact that the president appoints the prime minister, with the corollary that it is within his constitutional powers to dismiss him. By virtue of his long service as president under Salazar, Tomás is in the position of watchdog to the Salazarist heritage. It would not be inaccurate to say that since that autumn of 1968, the relationship between the offices of president and prime minister have been subtly transformed.

The present prime minister, Professor Marcello Caetano, is a man to be reckoned with, standing head and shoulders above the other figures on the political scene. A distinguished legist and a brilliant teacher before he took office, he is also a subtle politician, yet with qualities that make people like and trust him. He comes from a middle-class background, the son of a primary school teacher. He made a name for himself in his youth as a right-wing Catholic writer, and at the age of only twenty-three he was legal adviser to the Finance Ministry under Salazar and played a major role in drafting the legal instruments of the New State, notably the administrative code.

After a period as president of the Corporate Chamber, he entered the government in 1958, but was dropped after the Delgado presidential campaign of that year, and returned to private practice and academic life. Despite his staunch Salazarist background, he was strong enough to stand by his principles, as he demonstrated in 1959 when he resigned his post as rector of Lisbon University in protest against police action in the university precincts. During the last years of Salazar he remained an important figure in the wings of the political stage, although taking no active part in politics, and continued to teach and practise law until appointed premier by President Tomás in 1968.

Caetano is a Salazarist in his political ideas; in his advocacy of the corporate state as the answer to parliamentary democracy, his strong Catholicism, and his fear of communism at home and abroad as the major threat to the Christian civilization of the West. There are strong similarities between the thought of the two men, but there are also important differences. Salazar once said, 'Immobility is terrible. But to exchange order for chaos is worse.' He never seemed to envisage a third alternative. In his first speech on taking office in September 1968, Caetano looked cautiously towards a middle-of-the-road solution. He took as his slogan *evolução na continuidade*, 'evolution within continuity', implying change within the broad framework of the Salazarist system. 'Continuity', he said, 'implies a notion of movement, sequence and adaptation. Faithfulness to the doctrine brilliantly taught by Dr Salazar should not be confused with stubborn adherence to formulae or solutions that he at some time may have adopted.'

While calming conservative fears by pledging himself to continue Salazar's stand on communism at home – 'maintaining our national independence'– and the defence of the African provinces overseas, and stressing the importance of public order, he seemed to be offering an *abertura* or opening to the liberals. He emphasized the need for material progress for all Portuguese and promised to seek popular support through information, pleading for a reciprocal tolerance of ideas – from which communism was specifically excluded. In the context of the Portuguese political climate it was a skilful performance, and the elections to the National Assembly which followed in 1969 were a personal triumph for Caetano.

The liberal measures which Caetano inaugurated during his first year in office – lightening of press censorship, regularization of the legal position of clandestine emigrants, widening of electoral suffrage, and the abolition of the previous law demanding government approval for elected trade-union representatives – encouraged a number of bright young liberals to take part in the election under the then *União Nacional* banner. The elections were the freest to be held since the inauguration of the New State, within the limits set out by the 1933 Constitution. For the first time the opposition groups took part in the election campaign right up to the balloting, instead of retiring in protest at government limitations on their access to the electorate. They were allowed to hold meetings and press conferences and issue manifestos without harassment, and their delegates were invited to scrutinize the balloting. The voting figures indicate the depth of political apathy in Portugal induced by the experiences of previous years: out of a total metropolitan population of nine million, only 1,667,839 had bothered to register as electors. In the circumstances therefore, the voting figures were not unsatisfactory with just over one million people actually going to the polls. The *União Nacional* won overwhelmingly as usual with ninety per cent of the votes, but the opposition groups agreed that, in contrast to previous years, they had at least been allowed to present their case.

In 1969, after a year in power and a successful election, Caetano enjoyed the maximum credit with Portuguese public opinion, a credit which he had deliberately asked for on taking office, and which a leading Lisbon daily had warned him was not unlimited and must be justified. He had raised the hopes of the liberals and to some extent the fears of the conservatives. While Salazar dominated Portugal absolutely, Caetano has to tread a political tightrope between the two factions, the hardliners and the progressives, modernizing Portugal while at the same time avoiding antagonizing the traditional Salazarists.

In the circumstances Caetano opted for the safest course; instead of putting forward an ambitious reformist programme which might have aroused concrete right-wing opposition, he preferred to confront problems in a pragmatic fashion. With priority given to the acceleration of economic expansion, he brought several bright young technocrats into the government, Rogério Martins as secretary of state for industry, Xavier Pintado, author of a basic work on the economy, as secretary of state for commerce, and João Salgueiro, a progressive Catholic economist, to be in charge of development planning. None of them, however, was given cabinet rank. Rogério Martins drew up a plan for a dramatic restructuring of Portuguese industry, and negotiations were opened for Portugal's association with the Common Market. Diplomatic initiatives were undertaken aimed at breaking through the isolation in which Portugal found herself. The dynamic new minister of education, Dr Veiga Simão, presented a thoroughgoing scheme for the reform of the educational system. The political police, PIDE, notoriously a law unto themselves, had their status reduced by being transferred from the Presidency of the Council, directly dependent on the prime minister, to the Ministry of the Interior. Changes were made in the structure and leadership of the conservative *União Nacional*, which was renamed the *Acção Nacional Popular*. At the same time a new group called SEDES was authorized, which, behind its label of an 'association for economic development' has undoubted political implications. Finally, reforms of the constitution regarding press censorship and the future status of the overseas provinces were laid before the National Assembly. Caetano's version of the *Estado Novo* was to be called the *Estado Social*, the Social State, demonstrating his belief that social injustice could and should be eliminated through the corporate system.

Two factions watched – and watch – the progress of political events. The ultras, the conservative Salazarists, want everything to remain as it was, are deeply suspicious of anything smacking of liberalization, political or social change, and take a hard line on law and order and student unrest. They see Portuguese Africa as an integral part of Portugal, 'one from the Minho to Timor', and tend to regard Europe as an alien continent from which, like Spain, only ill winds blow. On the other side, the liberals want to see Portugal brought

93

more into step with Europe, politically, socially and economically. While not advocating the abandonment of Africa, they would like to see the war brought to an end, at least from the point of view of metropolitan Portugal, with greater autonomy for the overseas provinces. It is the old struggle between the *castiços* and the *estrangeirados*, first joined when the Restoration ended Portugal's Counter-Reformation estrangement from Europe, and now out in the open again with the passing of the similarly isolationist last years of the Salazar era.

Within Caetano's own party in the National Assembly, the two factions contend for the votes of the silent majority, who tend to support the conservatives. It would be a mistake to regard today's Assembly as a purely rubber-stamp body. Even under Salazar major changes such as the Organic Law for the overseas provinces of 1963 provoked lively discussion, and deputies' opinions resulted in alterations being made. Today's Assembly consists of some twenty to thirty liberals versus a roughly equal number of ultras, who do not support the government on every issue, while the remaining deputies usually vote with the right wing, but not necessarily with the government when its proposals run counter to the ultras' views. While having to calm the fears of the right and the ardours of the left, or rather centre left, among his own supporters, Caetano has to reckon with the powerful establishment pressure groups, the armed forces, the Church, and the business élite.

The army has traditionally been the deciding force in Portuguese politics since the beginning of the nineteenth century; and its potential power has grown with the vast increase in the size of the armed forces occasioned by the war in Africa. It has always seen itself in the rôle of saviour of the country, the defender of the national honour against the corruption of the politicians. Significantly, every president of the republic since 1926 has been a military officer (the two prime ministers, on the other hand, have both been professors). While the captains tend to support Caetano's *abertura*, the high-ranking officers are generally conservative and, like President Tomás, are prepared to accept only a gradual softening of the Salazarist position. They are deeply loyal to the president, and some of the more brilliant and successful generals are not without political ambitions.

The traditional Church in Portugal, although less powerful than it is in Spain, still wields considerable influence. In return for his protection Salazar expected co-operation and support for the regime from the hierarchy, and dealt severely with dissenting bishops. Under the terms of the concordat, ecclesiastical appointments were submitted to him for consideration, and the Cardinal Patriarch of Lisbon, Cerejeira, was a close personal friend from Coimbra University days. Cardinal Cerejeira retired in 1971 and the Pope appointed as his successor a popular young bishop who belongs to a different generation of churchmen, while Caetano welcomed back the Bishop of Oporto, who went into exile under Salazar. But the hierarchy as a whole tends to be conservative, and government proposals for an extension of religious liberty – which included making religious instruction in schools optional – roused the ire of the Church. Liberal pleas for a repeal of the concordat with a view to the legalization of divorce for church marriages would seem to have little chance of success. Caetano, a devout Catholic himself, has been suspected of links with Opus Dei, the powerful Spanish Catholic lay order, and he may well be sympathetic towards its objectives, which aim at the Christianization and modernization of political and economic life through a form of Catholic freemasonry. In the context of the Portuguese Church, he maintains a dialogue with both sides, with the traditional hierarchy and the lay Catholic progressives.

Big business interests represent an extremely powerful pressure group, and make their voice heard in the government. It has been estimated that the wealth of Portugal is in the hands of some two hundred families, and of those two hundred, about a dozen are among the most truly powerful men in the country. The Portuguese business and political world is a relatively small one, and things are still done very much on a personal basis. This makes it easier for the financial and industrial dynasties to exert considerable influence, as for instance do the de Mellos of CUF, the *Companhia União Fabril*, a giant concern with an annual turnover of £150,000,000 and ramifications in industry, shipping, banking and insurance. The business élite is a close-knit group with interlocking connections in every sphere; banks may be owned by oil companies who also have interests in plantations in Africa, in manufacturing, or in newspapers.

The administration needs big business to develop the economy, and cannot afford to ignore their opinion, although the young secretary of state for industry has not hesitated to take on the big cartels and vested interests with his anti-monopoly legislation. Big business in Portugal, as elsewhere, tends to be conservative in politics, and to demand strong, stable government. Yet businessmen are also among the more forward-looking members of the community; in a public-opinion sample taken in 1970 a high proportion of business leaders – 43 per cent – saw Portugal's economic future as depending primarily on Europe rather than Africa, as compared with only 18 per cent of the general public who did so. On the whole the business community supports Caetano's expansionary economic policies, although some of the most powerful among the older generation take the extreme right-wing view on the African and law and order issues.

The pressures from the left are weak: labour is not yet a force to be reckoned with in Portuguese politics. Under Salazar's legislation the labour movement is strictly regimented, and strikes and lockouts are equally forbidden; industrial conditions must be regulated by collective agreements between the officially recognized unions, the *sindicatos*, and the *grémios*, the employers' associations, and disputes arising out of collective agreements are settled by industrial tribunals. Wage rises and the increasing labour shortage have improved the unions' position in recent years, and some of them have become slightly more militant. The Communist party is active in the labour movement, and there has been a certain amount of co-operation between left-wing students and workers in opposition to the regime, but unrest has been firmly dealt with, and the views of the labour movement hardly count as a factor in Portuguese politics.

What is the real political opposition to the regime on the left? All-out opposition is represented by the banned Communist party, whose avowed aim is the overthrow of the system. The party is active, particularly in the industrial suburbs of Lisbon, but not strong numerically, partly due to strenuous persecution by the regime, and partly to the traditional conservatism and political apathy of the population. Two radical splinter groups linked with the party, LUAR and ARA, have been responsible for bomb incidents, and Maoism has been a factor in labour and student unrest. But communism in Portugal is very far from attaining the position and responsible influence which it has achieved in France or Italy. Despite its coherence and dedication, the communist movement is too radical an alternative to the Caetano regime to provide a viable solution for most Portuguese.

The traditional liberal opposition outside the regime, the socialists of CEUD, whose ideological roots go back to the republican era, seem to be a spent force, out of touch with the realities of present-day Portugal. In the 1969 elections they obtained only 1.6 per cent of the votes cast in metropolitan Portugal, as compared with the 10.5 per cent gained by the more forceful CDE, an alliance of progressive Catholics and left-wingers headed by the distinguished economist Dr Francisco Pereira de Moura. This coalition, however, dissolved after the election, as the extreme left became disillusioned with Dr Pereira de Moura, while his more moderate supporters were opposed to the extremism of the radicals.

In terms of feasibility and potential achievement the strength of the liberalizing opposition lies not with the communists, nor with the old style socialists, but with the progressive Catholics allied with the technocrats. One of the most interesting developments in recent years has been the formation – and authorization – of SEDES (Society for Economic and Social Development), an opinion pressure group with clear political implications. One of the leading members of SEDES is João Salgueiro, a progressive Catholic economist, formerly on the executive committee of the banned Catholic group PRAGMA, and in charge of development planning in the Caetano government until his resignation. SEDES is primarily a forum for the discussion of economic and social problems with political overtones, and it is a meeting-point for intelligent debate on the issues of the moment, such as the educational reforms and the industrial complex at Sines. Some members of SEDES undoubtedly see liberalization as best achieved through social rather than political measures, as the outcome of a higher general standard of living engendered by a modernized economy.

Meanwhile, within the framework of the regime, the liberal minority in the National Assembly does hold a certain political initiative; by pressing liberal measures on the government they can bring them to public attention. While their projects for reform are invariably defeated by the conservative majority in the Assembly, the very fact of their existence as a group in parliament is significant.

In terms of money, power, influence and organization, the right in Portugal far outweighs the left. The threat of a right-wing coup has hung in the air since the early days of Caetano's premiership, although his strong line on Africa, urban terrorism, and labour and

97

student unrest has largely disarmed ultra criticism of his policies, and in 1971 he felt himself strong enough to sack a right-wing general who publicly attacked the government on the law and order issue.

Caetano himself is a middle-of-the-road conservative who rejects the labels of right and left. He has said,

> my action in government is neither of the left nor of the right... if confronting the evident need for reform in so many sectors of our national life...is left-wing politics, that will not deter me from following that policy. But if the maintenance of authority and the conditions which permit the defence of the nation's vital interest and of public order without which it would be impossible to live, work, and progress in peace, is politics of the right, then equally this label will not prevent me from putting them into practice.

He has learnt from his master Salazar the value of a sibylline stance in Portuguese politics. By keeping his own counsel and eschewing ambitious projects of reform, he has avoided a direct confrontation with forces powerful enough to destroy him. Critics have also accused him of conjuring with words, of striking reformist attitudes which are not translated into action. 'Portugal today lives primarily on words,' a Spanish journalist wrote in 1971, 'the New State of Salazar is now the Social State of Caetano. The *União Nacional*... calls itself the *Acção Nacional Popular*. Censorship will soon be transformed into "previous examination". And even the feared, legendary PIDE – political police – has changed its name (it is now the DGS, Direcção-Geral de Segurança). Does the Portuguese evolution consist of anything more than words?'

Portugal remains basically an authoritarian régime as it was under Salazar; Caetano's moves towards political liberalization have lightened the atmosphere rather than changed the situation. The PIDE is still active, although its status has been reduced, and people accused of subversion can still be held for from three to six months without trial. Censorship of the press has been lightened, but not abolished, and the government press law specifically leaves the imposition of 'previous examination' to the discretion of the government. In fact the right wing have used what they call 'the state of subversion' in Africa to pressurize the government into declaring an emergency situation which necessarily implies censorship, while there has been an increasing tendency on the part of conservative business elements towards gaining financial control of the press.

However, while politically the '*abertura*' appears to have been more psychological than real, and the authoritarian framework of the regime remains, the government's attitude is considerably less rigid than it was under Salazar. The comparative freedom of the 1969 elections, the number of liberals within the ranks of the ANP who, despite their disappointment, are still determined to support Caetano, and the authorization of SEDES, all point to a more relaxed posture on questions which were previously considered beyond discussion. The outbreak of urban terrorism and continued student and labour unrest in the early seventies undoubtedly provoked a swing to the right. Caetano is not prepared to risk the political stability of the regime in which he believes. He has not, however, abandoned the social and economic initiatives which he pledged himself to undertake. Progress has been slow in some fields – the new industrial legislation came up against strong lobbying from traditional business interests, and dilatoriness in fulfilling promises of improved pay conditions for teachers led to a token strike – but nonetheless much has been done.

Reform has come slowly, but it has come, and from the top. It must be remembered that in Portugal, where politically informed public opinion practically does not exist, reforming currents can only come from above, from the dominant classes or the executive power. It is, therefore, the more to his credit that Caetano has realized the urgent need for social and economic reform, and that he has taken important initiatives in this field.

Popularly known simply as 'Marcello' (no one would have dreamed of calling Salazar 'António'), Caetano has inaugurated a new style of government in Portugal. In contrast to the remote austerity of Salazar, who reigned invisible behind the high walls of his house in Lisbon from which he rarely emerged, Caetano is smiling, easily accessible. He likes to move around among the people on impromptu tours, making himself known and gaining a first-hand knowledge of problems and opinions. His political style resembles that of an American president rather than a dictator; friendly, informal, approachable, he refrains from striking attitudes. He maintains a direct, personal touch in government, keeping his lines of communication open with people of different political opinions from the right-wing ultras to the progressive Catholics, many of them friends from university days.

Caetano needs to make himself known to the Portuguese people if he is to carry out his objectives. Between the pressures from right and left, he aims at the centre, at obtaining the freedom of action to achieve his 'evolution within the continuity'. To do this he has attempted to call into being a third force to balance the ultras and the reformers, to create for himself a broad base of popular support and moderate opinion. At his inauguration he promised to seek popular support for his policies through information, and to establish communication between government and nation. In contrast to Salazar's rare pedagogic dissertations over the wireless, Caetano initiated a series of televised fireside chats, in which he explained major problems and related government decisions in understandable terms. He has attempted to rouse the Portuguese people as a whole to take an interest in public life and the running of their country, to awaken the silent majority to a sense of responsibility for their own destiny after the long years of tutelage. By occupying the middle ground and mobilizing moderate opinion as a counterweight to the extremists on both wings, he hopes to achieve his objectives, evolution with continuity, modernization within the system.

12   Modernization and change

ECONOMIC EXPANSION is the key to a higher standard of living and the social welfare of the Portuguese; the administration has made it the primary target. Portugal is developing as an industrial country; her economy, once heavily dependent on traditional sectors such as farming, fishing and mining, is being transformed, switching the emphasis to industry.

There are many problems to be faced. Although Portugal's *per capita* income has doubled since 1961, it is still the lowest in Europe, and her state of industrial development is far behind that of the countries to the north. Progress in this field has been slower than in other southern European countries which commenced their post-war economic effort at more or less the same level. Portugal missed out on the economic miracles achieved by Spain and Italy; her indices of industrial progress – *per capita* consumptio of energy and steel, chemicals and cement – fall behind other southern European countries such as Greece.

Future economic conditions in a Europe dominated by an expanding EEC make acceleration of the growth and modernization of the Portuguese economy an even more pressing problem. Portugal will have to fight hard to keep up and hold her own. The task is not impossible; the basic infrastructures are there, plus Salazar's most valuable bequest, a climate of financial stability based on huge foreign reserves. These resources, the fruit of long years of careful housekeeping, are now equivalent to more than the cost of one year's imports. With the regular surplus on the balance of payments, they provide the fuel to launch a planned expansion of the economy.

One of the major problems facing the government in its effort to increase the growth rate is the poor performance of Portuguese agriculture. Over the ten years from 1960 to 1970 the average growth rate of the GNP was 6.3 per cent; and, while the average increase for industry was 8.6 per cent, reaching a peak of 13 per cent in 1964, the agricultural sector, with an average of 1.3 per cent, hardly expanded at all, and actually declined in years of bad harvests. Low agricultural productivity affects the balance of payments: after poor harvests in 1970, for instance, Portugal had to spend about $100,000,000 on food imports.

Portugal is still a country of peasants and fishermen, despite the growth of industrialization in recent years. In 1970, 30 per cent of the population was employed in agriculture, although it contributed only 15 per cent of the GNP. The agrarian problem is not new – it is almost as old as the country itself – and Prime Minister Caetano has rightly described the chronic state of crisis as 'endemic'. But although many of the difficulties that agriculture is experiencing at present are the same as those of the past, modern economic conditions have accentuated the situation. Internally, agriculture is feeling the impact of developments that are going on in other sectors of the economy, while externally it has to face the prospect of tough competition with more advanced agricultures, particularly in relation to the EEC.

The basic defects of Portuguese agriculture are the traditional backwardness and conservatism of techniques of cultivation, over-dependence on certain primary products for which there has been an over-all fall in demand, antiquated systems of marketing and distribution, and, above all, the structural defects of the landholding system.

The pattern of land distribution dates back to Portugal's earliest history, the *minifundia* of the over-populated County of Portugal in the north, and in the south the *latifundia*, the heritage of Crown donations to the Church, the military orders, the great barons. In most parts of the country the farms are too small and made up of too many non-contiguous holdings to allow integrated farming and rational rotation of crops, while in the south the huge estates stand in the way of a more intensive cultivation. Fifty per cent of the farms in Portugal are less than 2½ acres in size, while 95 per cent, occupying one-third of the agricultural area, count as small, i.e. up to 25 acres. Forty per cent of the land area is taken up by large estates of more than 500 acres. Only one-twentieth of the holdings can be considered to be medium-sized, and they cover less than one-third of cultivable land. Excessive fragmentation is illustrated by the fact that only one-quarter of the farms are composed of contiguous holdings, while one-third of them consist of six or more separate pieces of land; and although the average size of a farm is about twenty acres the average size of an individual holding is only 1.4 acres, and in the northern districts of Viana do Castelo, Vila Real and Viseu, they are probably much smaller.

The intense conservatism of Portuguese farmers both in techniques and in their attitude to their land has been a major stumbling-block to government efforts at modernization. Land is regarded as an heirloom rather than a means of production. Given the nature of Portuguese society, no one has dared to move towards expropriation of large estates, while attempts to induce peasant farmers to rationalize their holdings have met with scant success. Technical assistance, subsidies for mechanization, increased production of fertilizers, wine co-operatives, and vast irrigation schemes like the Alentejo project have helped increase productivity, but progress has been slow.

Historically, agriculture has suffered from government neglect; capitalism flourished in the nineteenth-century liberal era, but the rural areas were ignored. Even under Salazar, despite or perhaps because of his small-farming background, agricultural reform took a back seat. When Caetano's planners came to take a close look at the economy it became obvious that low agricultural productivity represented a major drag on economic progress, in terms of the growth rate and the balance of payments. Expansion in other sectors only worsened the problem; increased consumption caused by rising living standards and a booming tourist industry made demands on the food supply which the methods of production and distribution were unable to meet, and consequently led to increased volume of food imports.

In his basic work on the Portuguese economy published in 1964, Xavier Pintado, secretary of state for commerce under Caetano, pointed to two underlying causes for this situation: inelasticity of supply to demand, and inadequate systems of marketing and distribution. Portuguese agriculture, heavily reliant on traditional products – wheat, olive oil, cork, rice – has proved slow to adjust to modern market demands at home and abroad. Part of the blame for this can be laid at the door of the policies of the Salazar era which operated in favour of traditional crops as opposed to animal produce. The wheat campaign of the thirties encouraged the utilization of marginal unproductive land for the cultivation of cereals, guaranteed prices and subsidies favoured wheat, rice, olive oil and wine which would otherwise have been affected by market factors, while price controls on meat discouraged stock-farming.

The Third Development Plan (1968-1973) made the increase of agricultural productivity an important policy target and there are encouraging signs that production is beginning to adjust to the demands of the developing economy. While the traditional products vacillated with annual climatic conditions, meat production rose by 50 per cent between 1960 and 1969 and milk by 75 per cent. Fruit-growing, for which the Portuguese soil and climate are particularly adapted, showed a considerable increase; and new industries aimed at the export market were introduced, such as the processing of tomato products. Portugal produces two-thirds of the world's cork, and resin is one of her major exports; alongside these traditional products a policy of concentration on forestry as a means of utilizing unproductive land has met with considerable success. Eucalyptus, which grows well on poor, sandy soil, has provided raw material for new paper-pulp and cellulose industries, while exports of wood, and wood products, have expanded. The government has made serious efforts to rationalize distribution of agricultural produce, notably with regard to meat. The Alentejo Irrigation scheme, begun under the Second Development Plan and now well under way, projects the transformation of parts of the Alentejo into pilot areas growing demand crops such as fruit and vegetables.

The social consequences of the stagnation of agriculture and the pitifully low wages which were its result, were dramatically revealed by the census of 1970. Figures showed that over the ten years between 1960 and 1970, the nine essentially agricultural provinces of metropolitan Portugal lost 19.4 per cent of their population through emigration to industrial areas and to the developed economies of northern Europe. While in 1960 41 per cent of the population worked on the land, the figure for 1970 had dropped to 30 per cent. The labour shortage and the sharp wage rises which this has produced are having their effect on the modernization of agriculture. The pace, hitherto painfully slow, should accelerate as improved techniques and more economic methods are forced on farmers, with an increase in mechanization, and a trend away from the traditional uneconomic crops towards produce for which there is a rising demand.

The fishing industry is another traditional sector of economic life which has reacted slowly to changing conditions, and is passing through a period of crisis. Despite the paucity of harbours, the prevailing westerly winds, and a coastline open to the Atlantic swells, the Portuguese have always been intrepid fishermen. They were among the first to fish the Newfoundland banks for cod, and their fishing fleet still departs each spring for nine hard months in the North Atlantic. Nowhere in Europe is fish so much a staple of the people's diet, and the products of Portugal's canneries are world-famous. But courage, quality and tradition have not been enough to save the industry from crisis; the volume of catches has actually decreased between 1960 and 1970. The failure of the industry to adopt new techniques has been largely responsible for this situation. Since the mid-1960's the sardine shoals have been swimming further south into the Atlantic, far enough from the mainland to necessitate the use of larger vessels to pursue them. Falling catches, rising labour costs, and the price of tin cans in Portugal have contributed to the present difficulties of the canning industry. The government has reacted to the situation with fiscal legislation offering tax benefits to trawler and factory owners who amalgamate in an effort to restructure the industry into more economically viable units. Marketing conditions have been improved with the abolition of antiquated dues and the construction of cold-storage facilities, with distribution by refrigerated trucks.

The crises in the traditional sectors of the economy are symptomatic of the great changes which the country is experiencing, changes which are revolutionizing the social and economic structures of centuries. Portugal is in the process of industrialization after eight hundred years as a primarily pastoral nation of farmers and fishermen. While the metamorphosis of the old activities has been painful, slow, and long-drawn-out, progress in the industrial sector has been comparatively rapid. Growth rates for industry have been high over the last decade, particularly in the energy field which benefited from the priority given it under Salazar's development plans, and which has increased by 140 per cent since 1960. Manufacturing has increased spectacularly over the same period, with a volume growth of 128.5 per cent, mainly due to the introduction of new industries:

the steel works, *Siderurgia Nacional,* at Seixal on the south bank of the Tagus, motor assembly and manufacturing plants, synthetic fibres, cellulose products and tomato processing.

Shipbuilding and repairing has been a major new growth industry since the mid-1960's. Sixty-five per cent of the world's tankers supplying oil to Europe pass along the Portuguese coast, as do 67 per cent of other vessels carrying raw materials. Lisbon's superb deepwater harbour sited on this busy trade route makes it a natural location for the industry. The coming of the supertankers and the closure of the Suez Canal have increased its potentiality. In 1967 LISNAVE, a Portuguese-Swedish-Dutch consortium, inaugurated the biggest dry dock in the western hemisphere at Lisbon, the only one capable of handling the biggest ships in existence; a new dock has been added with capacity for the million-ton tankers of the future. The enterprise earns valuable foreign exchange, since all but one-fifth of its business comes from abroad. A new shipyard designed to build supertankers is under construction on the Sado river estuary near Setúbal; when completed it will be the only yard outside Japan to build ships of this size.

An accelerated industrial expansion and increased investment are vital to the economy. The principal problems in this field have been the fragmentation of local industry, the lack of technological research and know-how, a tradition of featherbedding inefficient industries behind tariff barriers with the concomitants of monopolies and restricted competition, a lack of entrepreneurial talent and capital, and a small home market – on a relative income basis the number of consumers in metropolitan Portugal is equivalent to only one and a half million western Europeans.

The government's reaction to the situation has been threefold: to rationalize the structure of Portuguese industry, to promote expansion and increased investment in productive areas by the use of selective credits and more state participation, and by attracting foreign investment. Under the industrial development plan the administration aims to mould small uneconomic units into larger, more viable ones, and to abolish restrictive monopolies and featherbedding. A more liberal licensing system for industry, the *condicionamento industrial,* has met with considerable opposition from threatened vested interests and the more conservative business establishments. Under the previous system established concerns were allowed to veto the setting up of rival enterprises, and the reform should establish a healthier industrial climate for Portuguese industry and foreign investment. An industrial development fund has been set up with powers to assist in the creation of new enterprises and the modernization of existing ones.

Nowhere has the retreat from the Salazarist position been more pronounced than in the field of economics, finance, and state participation in industry. The government aims to stimulate the economy by expansionary monetary policies, and to channel capital into priority fields by the use of selective credits. The official credit institutions like the Caixa Geral de Depósitos and the Banco de Fomento – the General Savings Bank and the Development Bank – which existed under Salazar, now grant loans to private concerns at lower rates of interest than the private commercial banks which, in the absence of a developed capital market, dominate the economy. Salazar was doctrinally opposed to state involvement in the economy beyond necessary public projects, but of recent years the government has come to play a bigger part in industrial development through direct participation in finance and administration.

Other measures to stimulate the economy include tariff reductions on the importation of capital equipment, and tax concessions for new industrial investment. Increased public spending has been budgeted for important infrastructures such as a new airport near Lisbon, a network of motorways, and the modernization of the railways. The most ambitious planning project in recent years is for a new industrial complex at Sines on the coast south of Lisbon. It will involve the construction of a harbour capable of taking ships of up to 500,000 tons, a ten-million-ton oil refinery with an associated petrochemicals plant, and a factory that will process locally mined pyrites.

Portugal lacks the capital and technical resources to fulfil her economic potential on her own. The regime has set out deliberately to attract foreign investment in industry, particularly in the setting up of new plants which increase exports and provide technical training for Portuguese workers and managers. For many years Salazar regarded foreign investment in Portugal with suspicion as a new form of economic colonialism, but his attitude softened in later years and by 1968 the promotion of foreign investment in the country was official policy. He had some justification for his views: historically,

Portuguese commercial opportunities have been exploited by resourceful foreigners, notably the English, since the seventeenth century. For a long time too, the resources of the overseas provinces were as jealously guarded from foreign interlopers as was the Brazil trade in the days of the *ancien régime*, and there were deep official suspicions as to foreign, and especially American, intentions towards Angola. Nowadays attitudes have changed, both at home and in Africa. There are some 1,400 foreign companies established in Portugal, of which 200 are British, with interests mainly in the growth areas like electronics, shipbuilding and repairing, cellulose products, textiles, and motor manufacturing. In Angola an American oil company and a German iron and steel group are among the foreign investors making the economy boom. The government has set up a bureau for the promotion and assistance of domestic and foreign investment.

Portugal has attractions for the foreign investor: a disciplined labour force, wages which are lower than the more developed northern European countries, an increasing number of university and technical graduates, favourable government policy, and a climate of financial stability. As Portugal draws closer to the EEC, it should prove increasingly attractive to foreign manufacturers who want to sell on the European market.

The diminutive size of the domestic market makes the Portuguese economy heavily dependent on external trade factors, and exports of goods and services account for a quarter of the GNP. Although exports from metropolitan Portugal have increased steadily in volume in recent years, imports exceed exports and their value has risen at the same rate. The negative effect of this situation on the balance of payments is, however, cancelled out by invisible earnings. Nonetheless, the trade deficit with the non-escudo countries is mounting – it stood at just under $500,000,000 at the end of 1970 – and the maintenance of a rate of expansion in exports is essential.

While traditional exports, wine, resin, cork and canned fish, have declined in volume since 1960, manufactured products, particularly textiles and paper pulp, have greatly increased their share of the total. Some 54 per cent of Portugal's exports go to Europe, which in return provides roughly 58 per cent of her imports. The United Kingdom and the overseas provinces are the principal markets for Portuguese exports; while an increasingly high percentage of her imports, around 33 per cent, comes from the Common Market countries. Traditionally Britain has been Portugal's biggest trading partner, but West Germany has overtaken her in volume of exports there. Within EFTA Portugal enjoyed tariff advantages to protect her nascent industry; with the enlargement of the European Community to include Britain, it is obviously vital that she should obtain some sort of association and preferential treatment to protect her developing economy.

Metropolitan Portugal and the overseas provinces together form the escudo area, which enjoys a long-term capital account surplus of some $100,000,000. Within the area, metropolitan Portugal has a surplus on her account with the overseas provinces, although this has declined somewhat in recent years due to her slightly diminished share in the export trade to Angola in favour of other countries, principally the EEC, the USA, and Japan. In fact, Portugal's trade with Africa does not follow a typically colonial pattern. It is not a relationship between an industrial power and its primary-producing colonies, but rather a relationship between two areas in the process of development. Portugal, Angola and Mozambique all have to import many of the same things – capital goods, chemicals, and base metals, for example – and nearly two-thirds of the imports of the African provinces come from outside the escudo area. The Angolan economy is booming, growth rates are higher than those of metropolitan Portugal itself, yet the provinces' total debt to the home country is considerable, well over $100,000,000.

Portugal's trade deficit with countries outside the escudo area is balanced by an annual increase in invisible earnings which provides a surplus on current transactions, namely from tourism and emigrants' remittances. Tourism has been one of Portugal's growth industries over the last decade. Although it has not expanded at anything like the rate attained by Spain, figures have steadily increased. In 1970, receipts from tourism totalled $222,000,000, representing a 33 per cent increase over 1969, while the number of tourists who visited the country in the first ten months of 1971 showed a rise of 17 per cent over the same period in 1970. Tourism has been given top priority under the latest development plan, but this does not mean that the Portuguese are prepared to see their country desecrated. The government's cautious, conservationist attitude towards tourism may have braked expansion and deprived the country of the spectacular profits earned by the Spanish tourist industry, but in the long run it is bound to pay dividends. The Caetano government has tried to reduce bureaucratic delays which have slowed the licensing and building of new hotels and tourist amenities, but it is not prepared to sacrifice planning control to unrestricted development. It is a wise attitude, since Portugal's long-term future as a tourist country depends on her ability to preserve the natural charm and beauty of her coastline, her landscape and her cities.

The other element in her invisible earnings, emigrants' remittances, has corresponded to roughly five per cent of the national income in recent years, and has risen at an average of around $50,000,000 a year – equivalent to approximately one and a half per cent of private consumption. While this contributes to the healthy balance of payments situation, there is another less happy side to the picture. It has been estimated that 1,500,000 Portuguese have found jobs abroad, compared with a labour force of only 3,100,000 in Portugal itself. OECD figures show that total emigration in 1970 was nearly 180,000, an alarmingly high figure in relation to a total population of only some 8,500,000. France, where in 1970 Portuguese represented over half the total immigrant labour force, receives the greater part of the outflow, followed by West Germany, the United States, Canada, and Latin America.

Emigration has always been a feature of Portuguese life since the sixteenth century when the poet Sá de Miranda complained that Portugal was being depopulated for the attractions of the East, and the seventeenth century when Severim de Faria pointed to the labour shortage caused by emigration to Brazil and the consequent necessity of importing 'Kaffirs and Indians' to carry out everyday chores. Perhaps because access to the sea was easier for them, the Portuguese emigrated at twice the rate of the Spaniards, who shared the same home conditions of a poor agriculture and unemployment, with more attractive outlets in the healthy uplands of the *conquistas* of Mexico and Peru. Emigration continued throughout the eighteenth and nineteenth centuries, becoming once again a source for preoccupation under the liberal governments. Alexandre Herculano defended the right to emigrate, saying that to oppose it was nothing more nor less than the desire to obtain agricultural labour at the cheapest price. In phrases that have a contemporary ring, he diagnosed its cause as 'the insufficiency of wages here', and added: 'the misery of one individual or another could derive from his own fault; the wretchedness that drives out from a country a considerable part of its population, already far from being superabundant, is always the result of a defect or a disturbance in the organs of society.'

While the defects to which Herculano referred, low wages and a backward agriculture insufficiently productive to support the working population, remain basically the same, the character and destination of emigration has changed since World War II. It has been estimated that of the approximately 1,200,000 Portuguese who emigrated between 1890 and 1940, 92 per cent of whom came from the north, the vast majority, 83 per cent, were destined for Brazil. Post-war emigration has been chiefly directed towards the richer economies of Northern Europe and North America where wages are far higher than they are at home; while a not insignificant number of young men leave to avoid military conscription for the war in Africa. In the post-war Salazar era, although difficulties were put in the way of prospective emigrants and clandestine emigration was severely punished, it did serve as a social safety valve, relieving the pressure of unemployment in the poorer rural areas. Nowadays, however, although many of the emigrants still come from those areas, an increasing number of those who leave are skilled industrial workers.

In the past, therefore, emigration has had beneficial effects: it has relieved social pressure through unemployment, contributed to a rise in wages and a better standard of living for those who are left behind, and forced farmers and industrialists to modernize and mechanize to counteract the shortage and rising cost of labour. However the numbers and quality of those who are now leaving present the government with a serious problem in relation to the future development of the economy. Prime Minister Caetano referred to emigration in a speech on television as a 'blood flow' that must be staunched. The government is not willing actually to forbid workers to emigrate, and the legal penalties for clandestine emigration have been lightened since Caetano's accession to power. He has tried to regulate the situation by international agreements: in 1971 an accord signed with France fixed the number of Portuguese emigrants permitted to enter the country at an annual figure of 65,000, while at home a programme of rural improvements aims to persuade workers to stay on the land.

A considerable rise in wage levels due to the labour shortage caused by emigration and the war in Africa has been an important contributory factor in the inflation which Portugal is now facing in common with the rest of Europe. OECD figures show that wages rose by nearly 12 per cent in Lisbon and 10.4 per cent in Oporto in 1970. The increases were not accompanied by a relative rise in productivity, and wage increases, particularly in expanding industries like construction, are outstripping rising prices. Yet the price of labour still accounts for a relatively small part of industrial production costs; rising costs, low productivity, and a dependence on imported equipment represent a greater problem for industry. Wage rises, the cost of urban housing, an expanding tourism and increased consumer demand due to higher living standards have caused inflation by putting too much pressure on the still old-fashioned structure of the economy.

Portugal has problems to face economically, but she also has advantages to help her confront them: large foreign reserves, a still-sufficient labour force, and an administration with expansionary economic ideas. Economic expansion is vital; the pressure is on, and she cannot afford to lose time. She must be able to offer her people adequate reasons for staying at home by streamlining her economy in order to afford the good wages, jobs and social benefits that workers in more developed economies enjoy. The success of the new phase of industrialization must provide a future for Portugal in terms of social change and the increased welfare of her people.

17 The Salazar Bridge over the Tagus, nearly a mile and a half from shore to shore.

18 The shrine of Our Lady of Fátima. On this hilltop in Estremadura, in 1917, the Virgin is said to have appeared to three peasant children. The flickering candles of thousands of pilgrims bear witness to the strength of Portuguese catholicism.

20 *Opposite:* Students, wearing the traditional academic gowns, in the main quadrangle of Coimbra University.

19 Salazar – remote, dictatorial, 'the volunteer of solitude' – never travelled abroad.

21 *Opposite:* Caetano – relaxed, approachable, 'Marcello' to all and sundry – seen on a visit to Africa.

22, 26 Fundamentally, Portugal is still a land of peasants and fishermen, heavily reliant on traditional products such as cork (*left*) from the cork-oak trees of the southern provinces, and rice (*below*, *right*) from Alentejo.

25 *Campinos*, mounted herdsmen of the Ribatejan fighting bulls (*opposite*).

24 Landing the sardine catch. With the shoals swimming farther out to sea, and the price of tin cans rising yearly, the industry is passing through a period of great difficulty.

23 Treading the vintage in the old way: this can still be seen, but is giving place more and more to automated co-operative wineries.

27 Telephone equipment assembly line in a modern factory. With the introduction of new industries, manufacturing has increased spectacularly over the last decade.

28 Representatives of a centuries-old tradition: port wine maturing in Oporto cellars.

29 The LISNAVE consortium's dry dock at Lisbon, the biggest in the western hemisphere, occupied by the Swedish tanker *Jacob Malmros*.

30 Every Portuguese citizen's dream of wealth – the seller of tickets in the weekly lottery.

13   Portugal and the world

PORTUGAL IN THE SEVENTIES is emerging from the isolation of the sixties imposed by the international reaction to her African policies. On the Portuguese side, the passing of Salazar has led to a more relaxed attitude to international relations. While maintaining the stand on Africa, Caetano has not the same exclusive obsession with the war. Rather he has realized the need for Portugal to make more friends abroad, and has profited by a generally more friendly feeling towards Portugal internationally to strengthen old ties and repair damaged friendships. While Salazar never travelled abroad, Caetano has visited Spain and Brazil, and attended the funerals of Eisenhower and de Gaulle. In 1971 the renegotiation of the Azores base agreement was the occasion for an important summit meeting between Caetano, President Nixon and President Pompidou. In the same year a British foreign secretary visited Portugal for the first time in ten years, and NATO opened its 'Iberlant' (Iberian Atlantic) naval command headquarters near Lisbon. Portugal is drawing closer to Europe in economic association with the Common Market.

Yet Africa is still the pivot of Portuguese foreign policy, and dominates her relations with other countries, although to a lesser extent than it did during the decade of the sixties. Although no longer exclusive of all other questions, it remains all-important. Any discussion of Portuguese foreign relations involves an appreciation of this factor and the reasons behind it. Portugal feels misunderstood internationally over Africa; her colonial experience over five centuries has been in many ways entirely different from that of other nations. The Portuguese do not see the African question in standard colonial terms; for them it is a matter of principle and emotion, bound up with their history as a nation.

Portuguese life has been intimately involved with her overseas possessions since the sixteenth century when first Asia and later Brazil absorbed all her attention and energies. Then as now Portugal's attitude to colonial enterprise was a mixture of God and Mammon, proselytizing and profiteering inextricably entwined. Prince Henry the Navigator sought to win lands from the infidel and souls for Christ while trafficking in slaves and gold dust; Vasco da Gama's men went to the East to search for 'Christians and spices'. The crusading missionary fervour which was burned into the Portuguese soul at the time of the Reconquest remains a strong element in the national make-up. The Portuguese talk of their civilizing mission in Africa, and, however anachronistic this may sound in modern terms, they believe it. Despite shortcomings in their colonial record, the inevitable cruelties and oppression, exploitation and neglect of their territories over five centuries, for them the crucial point is that they brought Christianity and civilization to those lands and thus feel a sense of responsibility for their future.

They believe they have a particular contribution to make to the world by the creation of multi-racial communities in their African territories. Much has been written about the Portuguese attitude to race, 'luso-tropicalism' as the Brazilian sociologist Gilberto Freyre has termed it. Caetano has described it as 'racial democracy, a great natural instinctive force in our relations with other peoples', and it is worth noting that, whereas religious discrimination was official policy since the Reconquest, racial discrimination was not. It would be an exaggeration to say that the Portuguese have no racial feelings, but they are less strong and less divisive than other peoples'. Undeniably they have shown a greater gift for peaceful co-existence and racial intermingling than any other colonial nation. Whether this ability to assimilate and live on equal terms with other races is, as Caetano claims, a natural instinct in the Portuguese character, or whether it has been historically bred into them through their long intercourse with non-Europeans is a difficult question. Since the sixteenth century when 10 per cent of the population of Lisbon were Negro slaves, the Portuguese have been more racially intermixed than any other European nation.

Portugal likes to point to Brazil as her great achievement in multi-racialism; and in her African territories she feels she should be allowed to complete the work that has been begun, to create a new Brazil in

Africa. Multi-racialism apart, they consider that they still have a great deal to contribute to the social and economic development of the provinces. The African territories need the financial and technical resources that Portugal is prepared to devote to them. In terms of human and economic effort, there has been a considerable outflow from the home country to Africa, particularly since 1961. It has been said that a statue should be erected in every town in Portugal at home and overseas to the nationalist terrorists of March 1961; their onslaught roused the Portuguese from the slumber of centuries. Since 1961 achievements in health, education and welfare have been considerable, and, in Angola at least, economic progress has been spectacular.

Caetano has called the defence of the African territories 'a sacred duty', a phrase which significantly recalls the fifteenth-century exhortation to do battle against the infidel in the service of God. The enemy which the Portuguese consider themselves to be fighting in Africa is not so much the black nationalists themselves, but the communist powers which are seen to be behind them. The infidel Moor has been replaced by his modern counterpart, the atheist Russian or Chinese. Caetano sees the defence of the African provinces in the same light as did Salazar, as part of the global defence of Western civilization against the communist threat. In terms of world strategy the possession of the Cape Verde islands off the West African coast and the ports of Mozambique on the Indian Ocean represent valuable prizes, and in Africa, as in Europe, Portugal sees herself as fighting communism in the defence of the West.

Portugal has always been aware of her ultramarine destiny: over five centuries she has looked out, not to Europe, but to Asia, Africa and Latin America; Spain barred the way to Europe. She has become accustomed to close ties with distant possessions, and considers that they have given her her position in the world. Psychologically, therefore, she fears amputation, the loss of prestige, the dwindling to a small nation on the edge of Europe, as she was five hundred years ago. A right-wing poster on the walls of Lisbon showed a map illustrating the size of Portugal with her overseas provinces as compared with Europe; the legend read: *Portugal não é um país pequeno!*, 'Portugal is not a small country!' It is only fair to say that this feeling belongs only to the extreme right wing. Their spokesman, the former foreign minister, Dr Franco Nogueira, argues that without Africa Portugal would be only a weak outer province of Europe, threatened with possible absorption by Spain.

Over the past decade, therefore, Portugal's entire diplomatic effort has been dedicated to the defence of her African policies. Old friendships have been strained, if not shattered, and new alliances formed, on the basis of international reactions to her ultramarine policy. When the first guerrilla action broke out in Angola in March 1961, Portugal found herself isolated internationally, and when India annexed Goa, Damão and Diu in the same year, not a hand was lifted to help her. Not that there was much that could have been done, for the defence of Goa against India was clearly impossible, but the failure of Portugal's western allies, and of England in particular, committed by treaty to the defence of Portuguese colonies, to help her in her trouble, caused great bitterness in Lisbon. Salazar never forgave Britain for what he considered to be her pusillanimous behaviour at the time of the Goan annexation. The Portuguese government's request for permission to use British airbases en route for India was left unanswered until too late. The Portuguese were deeply resentful of what they regarded as conduct unbecoming in their oldest ally, and the Goan affair put the greatest strain on the Anglo-Portuguese alliance since the Ultimatum of 1890.

The Anglo-Portuguese alliance has been the cornerstone of Portuguese foreign policy from medieval times, and neutrality within the alliance has been a cardinal principle since the eighteenth century. England and Portugal are each other's oldest allies; the treaty of Windsor signed in 1386 bound them to perpetual friendship. Historically the English alliance has been of importance in the defence of Portugal's independence, particularly in relation to Spain. English archers fought for João I at the decisive battle of Aljubarrota against Castile in 1385; English and Portuguese fought side by side in the Peninsular campaigns. Trading relations have equally been close since the time of Edward III, and there have been sizeable English colonies in Portugal since the seventeenth century. In Oporto, capital of the north, English families still control port wine houses with names going back to the 1670's; many of them have lived there for generations. In Lisbon too there is a considerable English colony, and English companies have long had large stakes in the Portuguese economy – the Benguela railway, the Lisbon transport company, and, until recently, the telephone system. Lisbon's buses, pillar boxes, and telephone kiosks are English; Britain still has the largest number of foreign companies established in Portugal and is her biggest trading partner.

The alliance was based on considerations of mutual interest – England appreciated the strategic importance of Portugal's Atlantic harbours, and enjoyed a predominance in her trade, while Portugal in return obtained the protection and friendship of a great power. On the eve of war in 1939 Salazar said: 'I have no doubt that from the British point of view the continuation of the Alliance should be examined, but only when the British Empire comes to an end, or when some cataclysm destroys Britain's insular position.' The situation which he postulated has become a reality: Britain's empire is no more, and her eyes are turned towards Europe. What will be the effect of this 'cataclysm' on Portugal's oldest alliance?

Anglo-Portuguese relations reached an all-time low during the sixties, when Britain was preoccupied with divesting herself of her remaining colonies and maintaining good relations with the Third World. In the prevailing climate of world opinion on anti-colonialism, Portugal was an international pariah, her friendship an embarrassment to any nation anxious to preserve a good image in international councils. Relations, already strained by Goa, were not improved by the accession of the British Labour party to power in 1964, and were tested almost beyond endurance by Rhodesia's unilateral declaration of independence. The sanctions policy requested by Britain and, above all, the British naval blockade of the Mozambican port of Beira, regarded as an unpardonable insult by the Portuguese, were the final blows.

The strains have eased in recent years, but with the break-up of EFTA and Britain's adherence to the Common Market, co-operation between the ancient allies is reduced to NATO and private trading. Portugal is still preoccupied with Africa, Britain with Europe. Divergent views over Africa, and English dislike of Portugal's political system, have weakened the alliance. Although Anglo-Portuguese trading ties are still strong, England and Portugal are less important to each other than once they were. However, interviewed by The Times in 1970, Caetano said 'When one reaches a certain age in life it is comfortable to keep old friendships,' and doubtless on that basis the alliance will continue.

Britain's membership of the EEC and the shrinking of EFTA led

Portugal to apply for association with the European Community which would give her a form of the preferential treatment she enjoyed under EFTA – i.e. tariff protection for her developing economy. Whatever may happen in Africa, Portugal cannot afford to be left out of Europe; although, given the different level of economic development between EEC members and Portugal, the differences in political systems, and her African ties, relations cannot be very close, at least within the near future.

Today Portugal looks on France rather than Britain as her friend in Europe; and ties with France have become increasingly close over the last decade. De Gaulle and Salazar understood each other and had qualities in common, not the least of which was a strong sense of history and its relation to contemporary phenomena, paradoxically combined with an unsentimentally realistic approach to people and events. France showed Portugal a degree of understanding of her African position; the French, of all the former colonial powers, have maintained the strongest links, not to say dominance, in their former African territories. Although historically Portugal and France have been diplomatically divided by Portugal's friendship with England, and the family relationship between the French and Spanish Bourbons, French cultural influence has always been predominant in Portugal. France is the closest European country to Portugal beyond Spain, and Portugal's first international railway link was with Paris. In the nineteenth century the French capital was the Mecca for fashionable and literary Lisbon society, a world described by Eça de Queirós in his *The City and the Mountains*, and it is still a refuge for Portuguese painters and writers today. Before technology and tourism made English the *lingua franca* of the modern world, French was the first language which most Portuguese spoke after their own, and although the young generation in Portugal tend to speak better English than their parents, French cultural influence is still dominant.

France has considerably increased her trade and investment in Portugal over the last decade. French banks were involved in the financing of the vast Tagus bridge project, and a Franco-German consortium won the contract for the huge Cabora Bassa dam on the Zambezi river in Mozambique. West Germany has outstripped both France and Britain as a major investor in Portugal. German money has partially financed the ambitious Alentejo irrigation scheme, and Krupp have a stake with the Portuguese government in the Angolan mining industry. The chancellor of the Federal Republic visited Portugal in 1968, and the two countries have signed accords for cultural and military co-operation.

Traditionally, Portugal's defence interests and her strategic importance to the western world have centred on her Atlantic position. Portugal is a member of NATO, and the Iberian Atlantic command headquarters are sited near Lisbon. Portugal is an enthusiastic supporter of NATO, which she sees as the symbol of western solidarity in the face of the communist peril, and is proud of her own rôle in that context. In the Atlantic, the Azores bases are an important factor in her relations with the United States. The bases are a vital part of America's global defence line-up, a fact which the Portuguese have exploited to their advantage. The government neglected to formally renew the agreement in 1962, to show their resentment at the Kennedy administration's hostile attitude to their African policies, although American aircraft continued to use the bases. As a symbol of improved relations with the US, Caetano agreed to a formal renewal of the arrangement, in return for American loans for development of education and infrastructures.

At one point in the early sixties a considerable body of influential opinion in Portugal saw the American attitude to Portuguese Africa as part of a Wall Street conspiracy aimed at divesting Portugal of her provinces in order that American business might have a free hand there. But with the changes in the American administration's policies, and the more relaxed and welcoming atmosphere towards foreign investment under Caetano, American business is making major investments in metropolitan Portugal and the overseas provinces.

Portugal's closest foreign relationship is with her former colony, Brazil. Brazil was the first foreign country which Caetano visited after taking office as prime minister, and the strengthening of the links between the two nations is one of the most cherished objectives of his foreign policy. The Luso-Brazilian Community, as it is officially known, is considerably more than the 'special relationship' which Britain once enjoyed with the United States; there is an official Luso-Brazilian Community day, and annual consultation between the respective foreign ministers. The Portuguese Constitution has been amended to give Brazilians resident in Portugal the status of

Portuguese citizens, enjoying the same civil rights and even, after a stay of five years, freedom to vote in elections.

The Portuguese are proud of Brazil, the multi-racial society which they have created in the tropics. Over more than two hundred years, from the late sixteenth century until the declaration of Brazilian independence in 1822, the colony in the south Atlantic was the pole star of the Portuguese economy. Brazilian sugar and dyewoods, gold and diamonds, gave the mother-country her commercial *raison d'être*. The royal fifth paid to the Portuguese Crown on the products of the Brazilian mines made João V the most magnificent of monarchs, and the Brazil trade, which the Portuguese jealously guarded from foreign infiltration right up to the early nineteenth century, gave Portugal under the *ancien régime* much of its importance in foreign eyes.

Even after the declaration of independence, trade with Brazil continued to be a staple of the Portuguese economy, and the principal outlet for her emigrants. In the history of Portuguese emigration, Brazil has played the part of the West in American imagination – as a land of endless opportunity. The jobless peasantry of the Minho, the Beiras and Trás-os-Montes flooded across the Atlantic in search of a better life, and the term *brasileiro* came to have a special meaning. In fishing villages on the nothern coasts or in remote towns or villages in the countryside, you will see some eccentrically ostentatious mansion of the late nineteenth century standing out among the simple stucco cottages like a cuckoo in a sparrow's nest. It will have been built by a *brasileiro,* a penniless emigrant who made good in Brazil and came home to dazzle his stay-at-home neighbours with his new wealth.

Some *brasileiros* returned home, many more of them stayed in Brazil. In terms of Portuguese residents, São Paulo is second in numbers only to Lisbon. The tide of modern emigration has turned away from Brazil towards the Europe of the EEC, but there are still close family ties between Portuguese emigrant families in Brazil and their relations at home. Brazilians and Portuguese share a common culture and a great link, their language, which is spoken only within the Portuguese world. The idea of a Community or Commonwealth embracing over 100,000,000 Portuguese-speaking people is a prospect which arouses enthusiasm in official hearts. 'Together we are a force on five continents, together we are a guarantee of the security of the south Atlantic, together we will be a culture that expands round the globe', Caetano declared on his official visit to Brazil in July 1969.

How much of a reality is there behind the high-sounding phrases? Politically and ideologically the two regimes have much in common, as they have mutual interests in the defence of the south Atlantic against infiltration by the communist powers. Portugal expects Brazil to support her stand on Africa; in return she is Brazil's link with Europe. But there is no escaping the fact that the two countries belong to different continents, and in the final analysis their interests must lie in the sphere to which they belong. The two economies do not mesh: Brazil is linked with LAFTA, the Latin American free trade association, while Portugal's economic relations are predominantly European. They are rivals in many primary products, notably coffee, although the common problems which they share in this field evoke a certain amount of co-operation; and both have developing industrial economies. However, since the Luso-Brazilian agreements of 1966, progress has been made towards financial and technical co-operation by private enterprise with government encouragement. In July 1969 the Luso-Brazilian Centre for Economic Co-operation was set up; in recent years there has been a merger between two of the biggest Portuguese and Brazilian banks, and considerable Brazilian investment in Portuguese real estate and tourist development.

Official enthusiasm for the Community is certainly strong; how seriously it is taken by the peoples of the two countries is another matter. Portugal tends to regard Brazil with fond pride, like a mother hen with her first chick, an attitude that the Brazilians find irritating. The Brazilian temperament is very different from the Portuguese – gayer, more outgoing – and there are many Brazilian jokes at the expense of the slower-witted immigrant Portuguese. However, jokes apart, a common language, religion, and culture do give the two peoples an identity as part of a Portuguese world, a tie based on the old adage that 'blood is thicker than water'.

Iberian solidarity is as important a part of Caetano's thinking as it was of Salazar's, and he has made at least two visits to Spain since taking office. It is significant that Spain is referred to in official documents, like Brazil, as a 'sister nation', while Britain and other countries are termed 'friendly nations'. The etymological distinction has a valid basis in fact and history. Despite long periods of hostility, Portugal and Spain have a love-hate relationship based on common

Iberian qualities and a similar historical experience. Although their paths diverged early in their history, subsequently they often ran parallel: both countries passed through the period of the Reconquest, that experience of winning back Christian territory from the infidel which so marked the Iberian psychology. Both knew discovery and overseas empire, empires which they had to defend against the powers of northern Europe. Both supported the Counter-Reformation, and shared the same social and religious problems – the question of the *conversos* or New Christians, the defence of the Church, the Inquisition, intellectual isolation from Europe. The bitter mutual hostility which divided them after the restoration of Portuguese independence in 1640 was largely wiped out by a common front against the French in the Peninsular War, and similar liberal experiences during the nineteenth and early twentieth centuries. The end of the liberal era in Portugal was almost contemporary with the defeat of the Republic in Spain, and the friendship of Salazar and Franco culminated in the *Pacto Iberico* of 1939, a cornerstone in the foreign policy of both countries.

Yet, despite all this, Spain has not been particularly helpful to Portugal over her African problems, mainly for reasons connected with Gibraltar and her need to stand in good stead with the Third World at the United Nations. On his official visit to Madrid in May 1970, Caetano appealed for Spanish understanding of Portugal's position, and underlined his view of the importance of Iberian solidarity in the struggle against communism. Portugal in Africa, he said, was fighting the same enemy as Spain had confronted on her own territory thirty years before. The two countries were, he said, 'united in the defence of our threatened culture'.

Caetano has many personal friends in Spain in the academic and political worlds. His second visit to Spain in 1970 was made to receive a doctorate from the University of Compostela, and one of his closest friends is Laureano López Rodó, a powerful figure in the Spanish political firmament and a moving spirit in the influential Catholic lay order, Opus Dei. Most of the Portuguese upper classes are bilingual in Portuguese and Spanish as they have always been, although the Spaniards rarely return the compliment – a fact which causes resentment.

Caetano's friendly attitude towards Spain and his desire for closer co-operation between the two countries are not shared by all Portuguese, however. The scars left by the Spanish annexation of Portugal in 1580 and a long history of battles between the two countries have not entirely been effaced. The Portuguese people as a whole tend to regard the Spaniards with a certain hostility and suspicion, and Spanish-Portuguese marriages are rare.

There is a popular saying, 'no good winds and no good marriages come from Spain', a relic of the disastrous dynastic marriages between the royal houses of Spain and Portugal which resulted in the extinction of Portuguese independence. Fear of Spain as a threat to national independence runs like a thread through Portuguese history from medieval times. It inspired the murder of Inês de Castro, heroine of a famous love story, the Spanish mistress of Pedro I, and the mother of his children. The same fear is still alive today despite the friendship between the two governments, and has been publicly voiced by Dr Alberto Franco Nogueira, the influential spokesman of the extreme right. Some businessmen resent the increased Spanish investment in Portugal that has taken place of recent years as a form of economic takeover. Portugal has nothing to gain, and everything to lose, by economic association with Spain, they argue. There is an unvoiced tendency to regard Spain as 'Big Brother'.

However, the Caetano administration does not share these prejudices, and maintains a firm desire for closer co-operation with Spain, particularly in the economic field. Both countries find themselves with developing economies outside the highly developed Common Market, both need to stimulate production and expansion in the face of international competition and the lowering of tariff barriers. Accords have been signed for Luso-Spanish co-operation in the fishing industry, and in the construction of an international bridge over the Guadiana river.

The situation in Angola and Mozambique has obviously defined Portugal's relations with the Third World, and with the African countries south of the Sahara in particular. The hostility to Portuguese colonialism of the Organization of African Unity (OAU) has meant that she has no formal relations with any black African state except Malawi, where Dr Banda is careful to keep on good terms with the powerful white states which surround him. But the more militant black African countries will have nothing to do with the Portuguese; their goal is nationalist victory in the three provinces of Angola, Mozambique and Guiné. They provide bases for the nationalist groups to train their guerrillas, and channels for arms supplies from foreign countries, including the Soviet Union and China. Recently there have been signs that the more moderate states like the Ivory Coast may be prepared to open a dialogue with the Portuguese, but generally speaking the Portuguese are isolated from independent black Africa.

Diplomatically, therefore, Portugal has relations with the white states, Rhodesia and South Africa. There has been a Rhodesian mission in Lisbon since UDI; Rhodesia borders on the province of Mozambique and the Mozambican ports represent her nearest outlet to the sea. For economic reasons the Portuguese would like to see the solution of Britain's differences with Rhodesia and the ending of the sanctions policy. The port of Beira in Mozambique has been badly affected by sanctions; with a total handling capacity of 5,000,000 tons it was working at a volume of 4,300,000 tons in 1965, the year before UDI – in 1970 the figure had fallen to only 2,800,000 tons.

Portugal's good relations with South Africa have not helped her in the eyes of the rest of the world. The government takes pains to point out that their relations are limited to common interests in the defence of the Indian Ocean in the face of increasing Soviet infiltration of the area. But Portuguese collaboration with South Africa over the Cabora Bassa dam project in Mozambique has resuscitated fears of a 'Zambezi line', a bastion of white supremacist states south of the Zambezi. Such a development would run counter to the whole tenor of Portuguese policy in their African provinces; the purpose of the dam is to facilitate the development of an area covering 54,000 square miles where 1,500,000 people live at subsistence level, and transform it by irrigation into a rich agricultural region. Until the Mozambican economy is sufficiently developed to absorb the total output, surplus energy will be sold to South Africa. Caetano has specifically stressed that this co-operation in no way implies approval of South African racial policies, and went out of his way to emphasize the importance of non-racist attitudes, what he expressed as 'our style of humanity'.

Portugal has regained a great deal of lost ground internationally since 1961. At the height of the anti-colonialist movement she had no friends; today world feeling towards her is considerably calmer. Africa remains her obsession, the pivot of her foreign policy, but beyond the Third World, the strain which it placed on her relations with other nations has considerably lessened.

Other factors loom larger on the international scene, the war in Asia, Soviet infiltration of the oceans, and the emergence of a more united Europe as a potential power bloc. New perspectives have opened up, offering a way out of her former isolation. Portugal in the seventies still stands poised between Europe and Africa. For the time being Africa absorbs her attention, but meanwhile behind the scenes the struggle has begun between the advocates of her ultramarine destiny and those who see her future in Europe.

14 Society in the seventies

PORTUGAL IS CHANGING; behind an outwardly traditional façade, important new trends are gathering momentum. Portugal is still a country with an extremely conservative social structure, and while radical political changes have taken place during her history, the anatomy of society has remained more or less the same.

Under the *ancien régime* a pyramidal hierarchy of king, nobles and clergy weighed heavily on the broad base of an ignorant peasantry, with a negligible urban middle and artisan class. The liberal era changed the composition, not the structure, of the pyramid: it created a new bourgeois aristocracy, in which big businessmen and professional politicians replaced the nobility and the churchmen in the seats of power. The disappearance of the monarchy and the democratizing tendencies of the republic offered the first real prospect of social change, but the revolution of 1926 resurrected the traditional hierarchic structure, albeit in a different form.

The establishment is still very strong in Portugal; government and big business rule the country, as they do in other more developed societies, and the mass of the population is passive. But beneath the surface new attitudes are developing, initiated and accelerated during the last decade. Industrial development, the growth of tourism and foreign contacts, the war in Africa, and emigration are effecting deep social and psychological changes.

The anarchist Bakunin once said of late nineteenth-century Italy: 'there is not one Italian nation but *five*. The Church, the upper Bourgeoisie, the Middle Class, the Working Class, the Peasantry'. In Portugal, where average *per capita* income is extremely low, the gulf between rich and poor is very wide, but is gradually being filled by an expanding middle class and a growing urban working class. The two nations within the country are not the rich and the poor, but the country people and the city dwellers.

The difference in living conditions and outlook between people living in the rural areas and residents of the major cities – Lisbon, Oporto, Coimbra, Setúbal – is a difference not only in physical circumstances, but in time. The peasants and small farmers are Portugal's silent majority; centuries of neglect by the central government have separated them from the experience of their urban contemporaries. Traditionally, the country people repaid the politicians' neglect with contempt and suspicion, an attitude shared by peasants, farmers and semi-feudal landowners alike. 'The countryside has been ruined by the lies of the capital,' the comment of an Alentejo estate owner quoted by a modern writer, is typical of their point of view.

Life in the rural areas has not changed much over the centuries. In the north the peasant farmer cultivates his minute plot, to which he is fanatically attached, with the same methods as his forefathers, ploughing behind oxen and making his own few pipes of wine. Every peasant has his pig which provides sustenance for the family for months; the annual pig-killing, the *matança dos porcos*, is a ceremony of some importance, when even sons and daughters who have migrated to the city return to help prepare the sausages, the cured and salted meat and the pig fat, which will keep the family in the difficult months.

Life has always been hard for the people in the remote northern areas of the Beiras and Trás-os-Montes, and in the Alentejo, in regions where the soil is poor and the traditional crops such as wine, olives and cork provide only seasonal employment for the workers. While the situation is bad enough for the agricultural labourer, it is difficult also for the small cultivator, owing to the uneconomic size of his plot, the backwardness of his methods, and his own deep conservatism. The government has tried to improve the situation by the *lei do emparcelamento* forbidding further subdivision of plots under a certain size, and encouraging the amalgamation of holdings. But it is hard to change the habits of centuries, and when a man's land is his only possession, each member of the family must have a share of it when he dies. The government has offered subsidies as an inducement to mechanization; but they are often used not to buy new-fangled machinery which the farmer despises, but a motor-car for the family; and, while technical advice centres have been set up, only the most dedicated agronomists are prepared to forgo the amenities of the cities for life in the remote areas.

Many villages are without electricity, let alone mains water or drainage; streets are unpaved mud tracks, medical and educational facilities inadequate, and amenities non-existent. But while this situation is not new, the disparity between rural and urban conditions, between ancient and modern Portugal, is becoming more and more glaring, and increasingly recognized as such by the rural population. They are becoming less and less content with their lot. Modern communications and television have opened up their horizons, education has given the younger generation a glimpse of a better life. The war in Africa has had far-reaching effects; young men who might otherwise never have left their native villages are conscripted into the armed forces; subsequently their ideas and attitudes are revolutionized by their experiences of the prosperity and amenities of cities like Lisbon or Luanda.

In consequence, there has been a major movement away from the land over the last decade; the total agricultural labour force declined by 10 per cent between 1960 and 1970. The figures for the 1970 census show that such traditional agricultural districts as Beja in the Alentejo and Bragança in Trás-os-Montes, which have no industries whatever, lost 25 per cent and 23 per cent of their population over the decade, while industrial areas like Paredes and Valongo in the Oporto district and Montijo near Setúbal gained 25 per cent and 27 per cent respectively.

The shortage of labour created by this migration has resulted in spectacular wage rises for agricultural workers, whose rates have more than tripled over the decade, but the drain on the rural labour force continues. Even when the workers do not emigrate abroad, they are not returning to the land. Factory work, even when not much better paid, is more attractive than agricultural labour, which is increasingly considered as lowering and inferior, and the amenities of the towns in terms of schools, shops and cinemas are incomparably better. Deserted cottages and land worked by women are becoming increasingly common sights in the remote areas. In the villages the women outnumber the men, many of them are the *viuvas dos vivos*, 'widows of the living', wives whose husbands have emigrated.

Rural Portugal, the traditional heart of the country, is changing, and with it some of the more picturesque old ways and attitudes. The Portuguese, high and low, have always been sentimentally attached to the land, *a terra*; generations of writers and poets from

Gil Vicente on have regarded the countryside as the repository of the traditional virtues of the nation, as compared with the *ersatz* values of the city. Simplicity, poverty, humility, the trenchant good sense of popular proverbs, represented the real strength of the people. Rural Portugal was the essence of being Portuguese; its traditions, Pascoães wrote in *The Art of being Portuguese*, were 'the primordial qualities of [our] race', as against the foreign influences so easily assimilated by the urban population. There is much to regret in the gradual disappearance of many of the old values and skills, the simplicity and frugality, the baking of bread and the treading of the grapes for wine, and the beauty of the festive aspects of rural life, the village *romarias*, the *festas* on saints' days. Yet the romance was also founded on the ignorance, misery and neglect of centuries which are only now beginning to be affected by social and economic change.

A universe in time and space away from what Pasçoães called 'my humble village of Poverty', Lisbon, the capital, dominates the country. Its population is the most advanced and representative of that other Portuguese nation – the city-dwellers. The city is growing rapidly, expanding in every direction to accommodate a mushrooming population. Migration from the countryside, added to the natural population increase, is putting considerable pressure on the housing situation here as in every other capital city, and rents have risen astronomically in recent years. Here, as in other countries, the cost of housing represents an increasing percentage of the cost of living, on the increase generally as inflation begins to hit the economy.

The average Portuguese head of a family works hard – he has to. Salaries are still relatively low, and nearly all salaried workers, even in the higher-paid positions, hold more than one job. This is so common that it has a nickname, the *biscato*, while the word for a cushy job or sinecure is a *tacho* or saucepan, which conjures up the image of a prosperous, well-covered family sitting round a steaming pot full of rich delicacies.

Prosperous or not, the Portuguese eat a good deal, particularly in the middle of the day. The average middle-class family will eat three courses – soup, fish or eggs, meat and a pudding. Fish in Portugal is the best and cheapest in Europe, although prices have risen considerably in recent years, and is still the staple diet, although the consumption of meat has increased with the general improvement in living standards. The national dish is *bacalhau*, dried salt cod, and there are said to be 365 ways of preparing it. On Christmas Eve after the midnight mass, the *missa do galo*, a dish of *bacalhau* is part of the traditional Christmas ritual. Portuguese fishermen spend nine months of the year on the Newfoundland banks to cater to this passion, but even then the *bacalhoeiros* do not catch enough to supply the demand, and *bacalhau* has to be imported from abroad.

A succession of foreign visitors remarked on the gourmandizing habits of the Portuguese; William Beckford noted in 1778 that his friend the old Marquis of Marialva, one of the greatest noblemen in the land, sat at table between two silver basins into which he vomited between courses in order to eat more. On the other hand, foreigners have always been equally struck by Portuguese sobriety. Drunkenness is rare; men drink very little beyond wine at meals, and the women almost not at all. Drunkenness is regarded as an Anglo-Saxon vice, and *bêbado inglês*, 'drunken Englishman', is a traditional insult. The Portuguese are very fond of water; Sunday trippers out of Lisbon go to nearby Sintra not only to eat the local cheesecakes, *queijadas*, but to drink the spring water from the Serra. The various bottled mineral waters from spas all over the country are very popular, and everyone has his own views as to which is the most efficacious for his particular complaint. As in France, the liver is an important and troublesome part of the anatomy, and although Portuguese cooking, unlike French, is on the whole not rich, their devotion to sweets made of egg yolk and sugar, *ovos moles*, may have something to do with it.

Cakes are a feature of Portuguese life, and nearly every town has its speciality – the cinnamon-flavoured custard tarts of Belém, the *pão de ló* of Alfeizerão, honey cakes from Madeira, the phallic cakes specially baked for the feast of São Gonçalo at Amarante. For women, pastry shops, *pastelarias*, fulfil the function that cafés do for the men, as social rendezvous where they meet their friends to talk about their children, their affairs, or other people's. Favourite hours for the *pastelarias* are mid-morning and afternoon teatime. The Portuguese are devotees of the tea habit – it was Charles II's Portuguese bride Catherine of Bragança who first introduced tea-drinking into England.

Statistics show that even traditional eating habits are changing. As the standard of living rises so the consumption of meat and dairy products increases, while the farinaceous foods, bread and beans, the staple of poor economies, show a marked decrease. The real poor in Portugal never ate meat, unless they were fortunate enough to have their own home-killed pig; their diet would be thick vegetable broth, or bean stew with a bit of pork fat, or rice with a sardine or a sprat. Nowadays the day-out treats for the more prosperous urban working class are the same as for their English counterparts – steak and chips or chicken on the spit.

The café habit is an integral part of city life for the Portuguese male, and cafés, unlike *pastelarias*, tend to be unofficially for men only. Although they have such a good climate, the Portuguese do not, as the Italians do, like to sit outside a café; they take their coffee-drinking seriously and the coffee from the overseas provinces is some of the best in the world. Mid-morning, before and after lunch, cafés in the city centre will be crowded with men in neat dark suits reading the newspapers, having their shoes shined, talking football, swapping the latest jokes. Jokes are a form of political outlet, and cafés are the grapevine for the news that does not appear in the press.

Cafés are part of male city life; in the traditional view the place for a woman is in the home, political and other masculine discussions being no concern of hers. Historically the Portuguese have a dominating, protective, almost Oriental attitude towards women which may well be part of the Moorish heritage. *Quem manda em casa é ela, quem manda nela sou eu*, 'she's the boss at home, but I'm her boss', is a popular saying to be found inscribed on ashtrays in any bar. In the traditional view women are regarded as inferior creatures: 'God created them weak', wrote the seventeenth-century author D. Francisco Manuel de Melo in his *Carta de Guia de Casados* (A Handbook for Husbands). Since they are weak by nature, it is only wise to keep them secluded, D. Francisco Manuel advised: 'There are men who readily show their wife to their friends. This custom is supposed to show simplicity of spirit and is used among foreigners; nonetheless the world today is not such that one would wish to be *that* simple.' Foreign visitors regularly commented on the seclusion of Portuguese women, and as if to emphasize the Oriental tradition, under the *ancien régime* the women of the noble class used to sit cross-legged on the floor on rugs. Even the nineteenth-century novelist Eça de Queirós, once a progressive liberal, agreed with D. Francisco Manuel's 'keep them out of trouble' principles when he wrote: 'to place a woman among her household occupations, that, we think, is the best way to avoid the dissolution of the marriage.'

In a traditional, male-oriented society adultery is only recognized as such when practised by the woman; a man is expected to have affairs. It was, and to a certain extent still is, quite normal for a man to dine at home with his family and then go out on the town with his friends to bars and nightclubs with professional girls. Businessmen who could afford it kept mistresses as a matter of course and a sign of status. Until recently the Lisbon demi-monde followed very much the same pattern as it had in the nineteenth century. By the same token of a belief in seclusion for females, actresses and models were considered, *ipso facto*, as prostitutes. Daughters of even the poorest families were kept strictly under control; sons of well-to-do families had their first experiences at an early age with the family maidservants. When it came to serious intentions, rich and poor went in for 'courting', the delightful word *namorar*, which rarely went beyond passionate glances and hand-holding.

If the woman's place is in the home, her natural function is maternity. Education was not considered important for a wife and mother; women should occupy themselves with the children, the kitchen, and religion. 'The best book is the pillow and the embroidery frame', was Francisco Manuel's opinion, an attitude that may account for the fact that there have been so few outstanding women in Portuguese history. No royal mistress ever attained the status of a Pompadour; Inês de Castro (who was a Galician), heroine of a tragic love affair with Pedro I, was a victim figure. There were two female saints, both of royal blood, Saint Joana and Saint Isabel, but no Portuguese counterpart of Saint Teresa of Avila. Yet the only woman writer of importance up to the contemporary period was a nun, Soror Mariana Alcoforado, whose *Letters of a Portuguese Nun*, written in the seventeenth century, were the reverse of Saint Teresa's spiritual flights. Banned by the Inquisition, they were direct, passionate love letters written to a French lover who had deserted her. In their pride, sensuality, frustration and yet lack of remorse they convey the cruel dilemma of an intelligent woman bound by the limitations of her society.

But society is changing today, and new attitudes are replacing the old. The educational reforms of the liberal republic benefited the generation that grew up in the twenties and thirties, and women have since distinguished themselves, particularly in academic life and the arts. There are brilliant university professors like Professora Virginia Rau, writers like Agustina Bessa Luís, poetesses like Sofia de Mello Breyner Andressen, and painters like Vieira da Silva, the most internationally known contemporary Portuguese artist, who works in Paris. Nowadays some 50 per cent of the students at Lisbon University are women.

Legally there is no discrimination against women in the labour sector, at least in industry. Under the Statute of Labour a woman must be paid the same as a man when she does the same job, although in practice women are usually employed for certain types of work and earn less. Women agricultural workers' wages are lower than those paid to men, although women do a great deal of the hard work on the land, and increasingly so in the present labour shortage. In general the legal status of women has improved since Caetano came to power. In 1970 female suffrage was decreed to be on the same basis as for men; previously voting qualifications for women had been more limited. Several discriminatory regulations in other areas were abolished: until 1969 married women were not allowed to possess passports or travel abroad without their husbands' permission, and women teachers had to ask the Ministry of Education for authorization to marry. Caetano invited a woman to join the government, Dr Maria Teresa Lobo, married with children, a law graduate born in Angola of Goan descent, who took office as under-secretary of state for health and welfare. In such a traditionally male-oriented society as in Portugal, her appointment represented a considerable step.

In 1960 one of Portugal's best-known contemporary novelists wrote a highly successful book in which he attacked the traditional attitude to women as symptomatic of a reactionary, primitivist society. It was in effect a plea for women's liberation, even quoting Betty Friedan. There is a generation gap in Portugal today: although children are still close to their parents, they hold very different views on sex, marriage and politics. Educated girls today are less and less prepared to tolerate the traditional *machismo*, the aggressive maleness of Portuguese men. They take jobs and go to nightclubs, just as the boys do. The majority are less advanced in their views and attitudes than their contemporaries in non-European countries; drug-taking and the permissive society have not really arrived. And, although there is a small hard core of Maoists, the political content of student unrest has been exaggerated. Much of it was the justified expression of protest against university conditions, together with a natural desire for more liberal attitudes on the part of the government. The scene began to change in the mid-sixties, and today's young generation are much more affected by contemporary currents outside Portugal than their elder sisters and brothers were.

The family is still extremely important in Portuguese life, to a degree which Anglo-Saxons find difficult to understand; it is officially enshrined in the constitution as the basic unit of society. All Portuguese exist within a network of family relationships – brothers, sisters, aunts, uncles, in-laws, reaching to the most distant degrees of cousinship. When a couple marries, they adopt the two family legions – the husband will speak of his wife's uncle as 'my uncle', of her cousins as his, and vice versa. Members of a family stick together, help each other, see each other regularly, and family events – birthdays, anniversaries, first communions, weddings, funerals – take precedence over all other social activities. Children remain close to their parents; there are few boarding schools in Portugal, and they tend to stay at home until they marry. Even after marriage a young couple usually see more of their respective parents than their contemporaries in England would.

Family stability undoubtedly contributes to the low crime rate in Portugal and to the relative absence of juvenile delinquency, although it does have its negative aspects. Writing of Mussolini's Italy in 1933, Herman Finer lamented: 'The great reformers, such as Christ and Plato, have always been dismayed by the obstructiveness of the family group in the reform of State and civilisation;... the family absorbs a remarkably large part of the thought and energies of its members.' The interest of the average Portuguese in the outside world is largely exhausted by the career of his relations, family obligations, problems, successes and failures. This absorption with family affairs may explain why the Portuguese are intensely patriotic, but not public-spirited.

Beyond the family society is a network of personal relationships running from the apex of the social pyramid to its base. The system of *compadres* and *cunhas* enables people to circumvent bureaucracy, obtain favours, or avert disasters for themselves and their families. *Compadres* are godfathers, who may or may not be influential, but the essence of the *cunha* is his position in society and the power he

142

wields. The word *cunha* means a wedge, a leverage to exert influence on the course of events. It is an institution that goes back to feudal days, when great noblemen protected their 'families', as their servants and hordes of hangers-on were known, obtaining favours for them and even protecting them from the consequences of crime. Even today the *cunha* remains an indispensable part of the business of survival in society.

Within the apparently hierarchical structure there is a surprising degree of social mobility. With education, intelligence, ambition and a skilful use of the *cunha* system, people from the humblest backgrounds can get to the top. Salazar himself is a case in point, and two of his most brilliant ministers came from the people: Adriano Moreira, the former minister for overseas, is the son of a shepherd, and Alberto Franco Nogueira, the former foreign minister, is the son of a policeman. The same is true also, despite the dominance of a relatively small number of established families, of the business world, and of course, the Church.

The Church still plays an important part in Portuguese life; despite bouts of anti-clericalism, Portugal has always been and still is a deeply Catholic country. Traditionally the strength of the Church lay in the countryside, where the conservative peasants and landowners kept to the ways of their forefathers and the parish priest was an important local figure. Rural life was bound up with the Church calendar; saints' days were village holidays, a relief from the hard labour of the fields and an excuse to drink, dance, fight, and let off fireworks. *Romarias*, pilgrimages to shrines outside the town or village, were the most important events of the year, occasions for the expression of a deep piety combined with a happy day out. The greatest expression of this quality in Portuguese Catholicism are the huge pilgrimages to Fátima, when thousands of people from every walk of life camp out in the open round the shrine. They bring gargantuan picnics, roast sardines on charcoal braziers, drink wine, and make friends with their neighbours, while at night the mass devotions on the vigil, when thousands of candles flicker on the hillsides and the singing swells in the darkness, are a truly moving religious experience.

The apparitions at Fátima in 1917, when the Virgin is held to have appeared to shepherd children in the Cova da Íria, were a symbol of the renaissance of the Portuguese Church. The corrupt Church of the *ancien régime* survived into the liberal era to become the prop of the discredited monarchy. For centuries the Church had been inextricably entwined with the State, an instrument of oppression and absolutism, the symbol of backwardness and reaction. Religion was rather a question of blind, fanatical devotion for women and zealots; any thinking man, however religious in spirit, could not but be disgusted by the corruption and cynicism of the reality. The onslaughts of the radical republicans which separated religion from the state and removed the vestiges of its temporal wealth, had a revitalizing effect. With disestablishment Catholicism took on a new, spiritual quality. Antero de Figueiredo wrote of the symbolical significance of Fátima: 'For years Our Lady of Fátima has been touching the hearts of the Portuguese people, from the humblest to the most cultivated, and, it would seem, particularly the most cultivated.'

The strength of the modern Church in Portugal is precisely its appeal to the educated. Attendance at church in the country as a whole is decreasing, particularly in the rural areas, where men rarely go to church. But while in the countryside, its traditional power base, the influence of the Church is perceptibly weakening, a process accelerated by the migration of the rural population, in the towns and among the educated classes the picture is different. A 1967 survey by University Catholic Youth showed that only 14.5 per cent of all university students described themselves as atheists or agnostics. *Cursos de Cristiandade*, Courses in Christianity, bring together men and women of all classes and opinions for days of intensive discussion between clergy and laity, primarily on social topics.

The modern Church is socially involved. From the practical aspect, nuns and priests do invaluable work in the poorer areas, in nursing, education, and charity. They run orphanages and schools, centres for practical education in skills like carpentry and domestic science, care for the sick and help working mothers by cleaning their houses. Priests are dependent on their parishioners' help for subsistence, they can therefore identify with the problems and living conditions of the poorer sections of the population. On the theological and political side, the young generation of clergy follow the most modern precepts of the Church's teaching, and the progressive lay Catholics represent the only serious non-communist opposition to the regime.

The Church in Portugal is passing through the same period of transition as in the rest of the world. There are the same conflicts between the conservative elements of the hierarchy and the younger clergy on political involvement, social policy, clerical celibacy. But its most interesting aspect lies in its intelligent involvement in social questions, the area in which it has most to contribute to Portuguese life.

But while the conflict between liberal and conservative, tradition and modernity, rages in political, intellectual and clerical circles, the majority of the population is interested not so much in political change as in joining the consumer society. With only twenty-nine television sets, sixty-five telephones, and thirty private cars per thousand of the population in 1969, it can hardly be said to have arrived for most of the people. But here again the gap between the country and the town is wide; Lisbon housewives shop in supermarkets and have washing machines, things unheard of in a Minho village, and while ox-carts amble along country roads, Lisbon traffic gets more frenetic every year.

The average *Lisboeta* leads much the same life as his counterpart in other European cities – working to keep his family, dreaming of sudden fortunes showered upon him by winning the *totobola*, the football pools, or the *lotaria*, the lottery. The buying and selling of lottery tickets is part of national life; wherever you go in the centre of the city you will be accosted by the vendors with their persuasive patter and streams of highly-coloured tickets. The different permutations of tickets are complicated, and the potential prizes large; proceeds go to the Lisbon Misericórdia, the oldest charity institution in the country. Excitement mounts through the week until Friday when the results are announced, just as, in England on Sunday mornings, people rush to the newspapers to see if they have won a fortune on the pools.

In Portugal too, the football pool, the *totobola*, is one of the most popular forms of gambling – almost the only one apart from private games of chance, since there is no racing, and gambling in casinos is subject to heavy restrictions. Football is the national passion, and the Portuguese have a natural talent for the game. The Lisbon club, Benfica, and its star player, Eusébio, are known all over the sporting world, and the World Cup competition of 1966, when Portugal reached third place, was one of the proudest moments in recent national history. Lisbon matches between the two rival clubs, Benfica and Sporting, draw larger and more enthusiastic crowds than internationals. The Portuguese are passionately and discriminatingly serious about the game; the crowds are quieter and less delirious than English supporters, and more objectively critical of the players' performances. Silence and even whistles can greet a Portuguese team in an international match if the spectators consider they have disgraced themselves; while they are equally generous in their appreciation of qualities displayed by foreign teams.

Bullfighting plays a far smaller part in Portuguese life than it does in Spain. There are no bullfights north of the Tagus except on very special occasions, and the spectacle, although beautiful in many ways, lacks the excitement of the Spanish *corrida*. Since the days of the republic, killing the bull in the ring has been forbidden, although he ends up in the slaughterhouse afterwards. In essence, bullfighting is part of a vanished Portugal which lives on in spirit; the *ancien régime* of kings, nobles and bullfighters, the reactionary world of Dom Miguel, brawling, brutal, courageous. The bullfight mentality is *machismo* personified; the Marquis, a character in Eça de Queirós' *The Maias*, exclaims: 'Take away the bullfight, and all we'll have left will be spineless mediocrities, crawling round the Chiado!' Another of the Maias' friends, the Englishman Craft, drawls, 'In this country, the bull should be what schooling is abroad – free and compulsory!' Mounted bullfighting was developed by the Marquis of Marialva, and a modern Portuguese writer has coined a phrase *marialvismo*, to describe the reactionary, feudal streak in the Portuguese mentality.

Bullfighting and bullfighters have always been intimately linked with the *fado*, as in Spain with the *flamenco*. Fado, which means 'fate', is essentially the song of the people of Lisbon, and the type-figure of the fado-singer is Maria Severa, *a Severa*, born in the popular Bairro Alto quarter of Lisbon in the early nineteenth century and made famous by her voice and her affair with the bullfighting nobleman, the Count of Vimioso. Words and feeling are the important elements of the *fado*, a sad, throaty ballad sung to the sound of two guitars, the Spanish and the twelve-stringed Portuguese. The popular quarters of Lisbon – Alfama, Madragoa, and the Bairro Alto – are the home of the *fado*, although Coimbra has its own version, traditionally sung by students, smoother, more melodic, but equally

146

dedicated to the sufferings of love. *Fado* is sung by men and women; but the greatest *fadista* of the day, and one of the most gifted of all time, is Amália Rodrigues. An exceptionally beautiful and intelligent woman, known simply as 'Amália', she once sold oranges in the Lisbon market, and is now internationally famous. With her insight and her art she has given the *fado* new dimensions, singing the works of Camões and the best modern poets set to music.

CONTEMPORARY LITERATURE

Poetry is the great strength of Portuguese literature, and the twentieth century has been one of its richest periods. The first three decades were dominated by the enigmatic figure of Fernando Pessoa, who, with the gifted symbolist poet Mário de Sá Carneiro, founded the first *avant garde* review, *Orfeu*.

Pessoa wrote as himself and as three other distinct personages, each clearly defined in attitude and style, Alberto Caeiro, Ricardo Reis and Álvaro de Campos. His work has had great influence on the modern generation of poets. It was he who once wrote that if it was necessary to choose only one word to define the Portuguese mentality, that word would be provincialism. Like most Portuguese writers and intellectuals he was perhaps over-conscious of this provincialism, a feeling of non-Europeanism, of being cut off from the mainstream of modern thought. Portuguese writers create for a small audience in a language that no one else in Europe speaks or understands, and for them this naturally poses a dilemma. The gulf between artists and intellectuals and the rest of the people, which exists in every country, is particularly wide in Portugal, and at the same time they are cut off by their language from response and appreciation by their counterparts in other countries.

Yet this isolation is in a way one of the strengths of Portuguese poetry; it has given it an intensely subjective, individual, national quality. There is an extraordinary number of modern poets of the first rank, Alexandre O'Neill, Sofia de Mello Breyner Andressen, Pedro Homem de Mello, David Mourão Ferreira, to name but a few; artists in their language, deeply committed to the problems and way of being of their society.

This quality of involvement in the life of their country is likewise the distinguishing feature of Portuguese prose writers, despite the difficulties engendered by censorship. Neo-realism came to Portugal

147

in the thirties through Hemingway, Steinbeck, Dos Passos and the Brazilian writers José Lins do Rego and Jorge Amado. Fifty years before, in the age of Eça de Queirós, realism had meant the portrayal of middle- and upper-class urban society, while earlier, rural life had been treated in a romantic fashion as in the novels of Camilo Castelo Branco.

For the new generation, however, realism involved showing the life of the poor as it really was, with the veils of romantic sentiment removed. The life of the agricultural workers, particularly in the Alentejo where the contrast between seignorial feudalism and the rural proletariat was strongest, came to represent the real truth of society's problems. A generation of novelists began to write about rural society, among them Ferreira de Castro, whose *A Selva*, written in 1930, has been translated into fourteen languages, and Vergílio Ferreira, who are considered two of the most important modern novelists. Aquilino Ribeiro, one of the best-known writers, although of an older generation and outside the main literary stream, also wrote of the countryside, often in the dialect of his native Beira.

Portuguese intellectuals tend towards self-depreciation, a literary inferiority neurosis. Two important figures on the post-war scene, Miguel Torga and Fernando Namora, both voice the age-old dilemma of the *estrangeirado*, that of being 'European in Portugal and Portuguese in Europe'. They are conscious of the limitations of their environment, and thus of their ability to communicate, and therefore tend to be pessimistic about their own talents. Yet possibly never before have there been so many good writers of integrity active at the same time – Agustina Bessa Luís, José Cardoso Pires, Maria Lamas among them. Portugal and the experience of being Portuguese is their subject; and it is through their sensitive, compassionate and intelligent comments on contemporary life that a true perspective of Portugal as it is today emerges.

15   The future

WHAT DOES THE FUTURE HOLD for Portugal, and how do the Portuguese themeselves see it ?

For most people, government and governed, the over-riding goal must be the modernization of the country, yet without the sacrifice of its traditional values : *cumprir o Portugal de sempre no mundo de hoje*, 'to fulfil traditional Portugal in the terms of today's world'. One may wonder if this is not a case of wanting to have one's cake and eat it, but the Portuguese are a tenacious people, and their own particular qualities may make this possible. Political, social and economic evolution are essential if Portugal is to keep pace with the modern world.

Politically, the issue is not so much the survival of the regime but the direction it will take. Contrary to many prognostications, it has survived the passing of Salazar, and has now existed in its present form for nearly half a century. Yet Portugal is changing and the regime must keep pace with the development of the country ; the question is – how will it evolve ?

Caetano believes in the theory of the corporate state and in its fundamental validity in the Portuguese context. Like most conservative and middle-of-the-road Portuguese he regards parliamentary democracy as unsuited to the Portuguese temperament and circumstances, and it is undeniable that the previous experiments in the democratic party system, although productive of beneficial results, did not work. The twin rocks on which they foundered were the lack of a parliamentary tradition, and the apathy and ignorance of the mass of the population.

The liberals believe that Portugal has progressed to the stage where a democratic system would not be the inevitable preliminary to chaos. Yet the majority are still politically unaware ; informed public opinion is limited to a relatively small section of the population, and any attempt to impose a truly democratic form of government would undoubtedly provoke an extreme right-wing reaction and result in an ultra-conservative dictatorship. Effective political change, therefore, must take place within the framework of the present regime.

Caetano, although temperamentally conservative, is too intelligent to be a diehard. He is also basically humanitarian. He realizes that, to survive, any system must evolve – 'evolution within the continuity'. He believes in the nature and theory of the corporate state, but would undoubtedly like to see greater popular participation in the action of government. The problem as he sees it is the democratization of the system without recourse to parliamentary democracy or party politics. The future may lie with some form of presidentialism, retaining the organs of the corporate state, but headed by an executive power elected by the nation. A president elected under those conditions would thus have a popular mandate, and a broader power base from which he could operate without being, as at present, sandwiched between the forces of right and left. The success of the system would of course depend on the stature of the man in power, and its validity on his personal capabilities and good will. It would, however, have the inestimable practical and psychological advantage that the leader could be removed if the electorate really wanted to dismiss him.

Meanwhile Portugal's political future depends on the continuation of Caetano's successful balancing act between right and left. The right, chiefly represented by the older generation, is still very powerful, but as long as the prime minister remains open to new ideas, the importance of informed liberal pressure groups such as SEDES should not be underestimated. The political atmosphere in Portugal has lightened considerably since the passing of Salazar, and liberalization of the regime should come with a higher general level of education and economic progress. The future lies with the younger generation, and their future depends on the success of present economic and social policies.

A public-opinion poll conducted in the spring of 1971 placed education as the most important problem facing Portugal today, seven out of ten adults of all classes putting it at the top of the table. Portugal's progress in this field has not been spectacular hitherto: the illiteracy rate has dropped considerably from an estimated 61.8 per cent in 1930 to 40.4 per cent in 1950, and around 15 to 18 per cent today, with 7.9 per cent of those under forty still illiterate.

However, the question today is not so much one of illiteracy, but of the quality and availability of educational facilities. The major deficiencies of the education service in Portugal now, faced with the continued rise in the school age population, are inadequate overcrowded school buildings, an insufficient number of trained teachers, and antiquated courses, entrance examinations and graduation systems.

The extreme urgency of reform is generally recognized. In one of his early talks on television Caetano spoke of the 'great, urgent, and decisive battle for education', and again of the 'reform of society through education'. Reform should resolve some social tensions; resentment at the inadequacies of the system was a major source of the continuing student unrest. Although some of the trouble was politically motivated, many of the grievances were real and generally recognized to be so. In 1967 the number of students attending the universities of Coimbra, Lisbon and Oporto totalled 30,056, representing only 0.35 per cent of the total population. Inadequate training and the meagre salaries paid to teachers and academics have contributed to the situation.

Improved educational and vocational training facilities are essential if Portugal's technological revolution is to be achieved. The new phase of industrialization cannot hope to succeed without suitably trained personnel in the higher and lower echelons, and the future of the country depends to a large extent on its success. With the exception of the engineering school, which has maintained a consistently high standard, technical training at the higher and lower levels has been lacking. In 1969, of the total personnel employed in industry, 64 per cent were workmen with no qualifications, and only 0.9 per cent were at managerial level, and of these managers only 18 per cent held university degrees. Despite the development of the economy over the decade from 1950 to 1960, there was no increase in the number of degrees awarded in subjects vital to industry, rather the reverse.

It might perhaps be unfair to say that Salazar regarded education as a luxury, but it is certainly true to say that he did not give it high priority. Today education is seen as an absolute necessity, the key to the country's economic and social development. The minister of education, Dr José Veiga Simão, is a brilliant Cambridge graduate in his forties and a popular former rector of the University of Lourenço Marques in Mozambique, and educational reform is being given a prominence it has not enjoyed since the days of the Republic. The reforms announced in 1971 represent the first general modernization of the system for forty years. They include raising the school-leaving age from twelve to fourteen, eight years instead of six of compulsory school attendance for all children, and two years of optional kindergarten school before pupils enter primary school at the age of six. Compulsory education will now cover all children from the ages of six to fourteen; they can then continue for four more years of mixed general schooling and specialized courses. Schools will be comprehensive establishments called lyceums, and pupils in their final year will be able to concentrate on a specialized course with a view to their future careers.

In higher education, university entrance examinations have been replaced by a final school examination; while entrance tests for the commercial and industrial institutes have been simplified, and the graduation system in universities which was formerly so difficult and intricate that comparatively few graduates actually obtained their degrees, will be reformed. Plans have been made to facilitate the entry of those over twenty-five into university, and there will be subsidies for post-graduates. Teacher training, pay, conditions and incentives will be improved, and teaching methods modernized. As an earnest of their intentions the government increased the budget for education to $175,000,000 in 1971.

Emigration ranks as a major issue in the seventies; the continued loss of manpower must be stemmed if the economy is to expand in the future. To do this, living conditions for workers in Portugal must be improved, not only in terms of higher wages, but in housing, public health and welfare. Housing was one of the issues of the 1969 election and came high on the list of problems in the 1971 opinion poll. Rents have spiralled in the capital over recent years, and the housing situation in the major towns has been worsened by the migration of the rural population, and by the fact that much of the new construction in the private sector has been luxury and not economy building. The government talks of plans for rural improvements as an inducement to persuade the people to stay on the land, and Caetano has laid considerable stress on the importance of improving their lot. Only by making rural life more attractive can the movement of population away from the land, to go abroad or to the cities, be reduced. In 1969 the Housing Development Fund was set up to co-operate with the municipalities and private enterprise in increasing the quantity of available economic housing. Public investment in this field has risen slightly under the Third Development Plan (1968-73) when $216,000,000 were budgeted for a projected fifty thousand new homes, as compared with $70,000,000 under the previous intermediary plan from 1965 to 1967. However, the percentage of houses built with public funds represents only between five and ten per cent of the total. Meanwhile rents rise and the pressure on urban housing increases; the problem of providing reasonable housing at economic prices becomes more and more urgent.

Living standards and social welfare generally are given higher priorities under present government policy than under Salazar. A larger proportion of the country's reserves are being deployed in social development; Portugal cannot continue for ever at the bottom of the European statistical table for education, health and welfare. In many areas figures compare unfavourably even in relation to other southern European countries and Spain. For instance the adult death rate stands at roughly the European average, but infant mortality is far higher and over-all life expectancy lower than the norm. There has been a steady improvement over the past decade: infant mortality which stood at the rate of 95.5 per thousand births in 1953 had fallen to 59 by 1966, while life expectancy for men had risen from 49 years to 60.7, and for women to 66.3. The average contemporary European figures were 67 for men and 72.3 for women. Tuberculosis kills nearly as many people annually as die in accidents on the roads, but a vigorous anti-TB campaign has greatly decreased the number of its victims. There are only some eight thousand registered doctors in metropolitan Portugal and, of that number, one-half practise in Lisbon and Oporto.

The high proportion of doctors practising in the two major cities as compared with the rest of the country serves only to underline the disparity between urban and rural conditions, and nowhere has this been more apparent than in the field of social welfare. Workers in industry are well covered by health insurance, pension and family allowance schemes administered by the *Caixas de Previdência e Abono e Familia*, the social security funds operated by the trade unions and the employers' representatives. Health insurance under these schemes provides free medical care, three-quarters of the cost of drugs, and free hospitalization. Sick benefits amount to 60 per cent of wages. Employees of the big private companies like CUF, the Portuguese equivalent of ICI, are exceptionally well looked after, with company schools, hospitals, housing and a number of fringe benefits. Civil servants, although less well paid than workers in the industrial sector, are also covered by state insurance schemes which have been extended in recent years. Social welfare in general comes under the Ministry of Corporations, which is also responsible for a nation-wide organization, FNAT (the National Federation for Happiness in Work), which looks after workers' leisure activities, organizing canteens, summer camps, sports, theatre and entertainments.

But for years the situation was far from happy for fishermen and agricultural workers. In theory the *Casas dos Pescadores* for fishermen and the *Casas do Povo* for rural workers were supposed to operate on the same lines as the industrial *Caixas* in the towns. In practice however, funds were poor, medical treatment inadequate, there was no proper provision for hospitalization, no pensions, family allowances or sickness benefits.

To its credit, the Caetano government set out in its first year in office to correct this glaring injustice. In 1969 family allowances were given to rural workers, and in the following year, invalid and old-age pensions and sickness benefits. In 1970, old-age pensions, family allowances and free hospitalization were extended to twenty thousand fishermen. Conditions for the fishermen and agricultural workers, the long-suffering *povo*, the people, of Portugal, are still not equal to those enjoyed by the industrial workers, but at least a start in the right direction has been made. However, there are still sections of the population who are not covered by State or syndical welfare systems, and who are dependent on the efforts of private charity, medical services, hospitals, schools and orphanages associated with religious institutions or the Misericordia organizations in the towns, and the parish councils. Caetano has pledged himself to correct the inequalities of the social welfare system, and has begun on a rationalization of the existing administration; a Superior Council for Social Action has been set up to co-ordinate the activities of the Ministries of Corporations and Welfare with those of Health and Public Assistance.

On the domestic front there are signs that the Caetano government has got its priorities right; in every major policy speech emphasis is laid on the need for social improvement and the raising of the standard of living. Economic expansion, it is hoped, will support the cost of these programmes in the future, but there is always a conditioning factor – Africa. The costs and implications of Portugal's relationship with her overseas provinces affects every other question in her present and future, both domestic and foreign. The war in Africa has gone on for over a decade, and shows no signs of ending. Can metropolitan Portugal continue to bear the strain in terms of money and manpower? Is she mortgaging the future of the home country to that of the overseas territories?

Portugal keeps between 120,000 and 150,000 troops in Africa fighting guerrilla action by black nationalist groups in her provinces of Guiné (Portuguese Guinea), Angola and Mozambique. In Guiné the nationalist group, PAIGC, is led by Amilcar Cabral, born in Cape Verde of a Cape Verdean father and a Mandinga mother from Guiné, and educated at Lisbon University. Guiné is not settler country; its 600,000 people live chiefly by agriculture, and the whites are mostly officials. The PAIGC can claim more solid successes here than can the nationalist groups in the other territories; estimates of the land they control range from one-third to fifty per cent, and within their areas they have established schools and hospitals. Cabral is a relatively moderate leader who would like to open a dialogue with the Portuguese. Although he aims at the liberation of the Cape Verde islands, he is prepared to envisage independence for the mainland without the islands, and has said publicly that he would like to maintain relations with Lisbon after independence. From the Portuguese point of view, however, although they have little to gain by staying in Guiné, its abandonment would not only encourage nationalist forces elsewhere, but threaten the security of the islands, whose strategic position makes them important within the context of NATO defence.

The picture is very different in the huge and increasingly prosperous province of Angola with its population of five million, nearly 200,000 of whom are whites, and whose capital, Luanda, is the biggest in population terms after Lisbon and Oporto. The war began here in March 1961, but since then the nationalist groups have made little headway, and their activities are confined to the border areas and based on the neighbouring African states. The situation is complicated by rivalry between the different groups, the UPA led by Holden Roberto, the MPLA under Agostinho Neto, and the

GRAE, based on Kinshasa and Zaire, by tribal differences and the vast distances between the border areas and the centres of population.

Angola is potentially very rich, not only in agriculture and fishing, but in diamonds, iron ore, oil and other mineral resources. The economy is booming, and a considerable amount of investment – public, private and foreign – is being channelled into the province. Included under the development plan is the ambitious Cunene river project, with a series of dams and planned colonization of the area at a cost of some $310,000,000.

The huge Cabora Bassa dam planned for the development of the Zambezi valley is the chief guerrilla target on the Indian Ocean. The main nationalist group is FRELIMO, which with COREMO and UNITA operate from Zambia and Tanzania against the northern borders of the province and, in the case of UNITA, against south-eastern Angola. The extent of the territory which they control in the north is difficult to estimate: in 1968 FRELIMO claimed a third to a quarter of the province, while a visiting news team from *The Times* calculated that five per cent would be nearer the mark.

On the whole, therefore, except in Guiné, the nationalist parties have made little headway over the past decade, either in territorial control or in terms of representing viable alternative governments. Yet the essential fact from the point of view of metropolitan Portugal is that they have succeeded in forcing the central government to deploy a large army at an increasingly escalating cost.

In recent years, extraordinary military expenditure, i.e. the African wars, has accounted for up to 30 per cent of the central government budget as compared with only 13 per cent ordinary military expenditure. At that rate nearly half Portugal's annual budget is devoted to defence, a heavy burden for any country to bear. It is impossible to calculate accurately how much she gains in return. Portuguese Africa is important to Portugal's foreign trade, absorbing a considerable proportion of her exports, but the provinces are also in debt to the home country, and the balance of trade between Portugal and the overseas provinces is unimportant in relation to metropolitan Portugal's over-all balance-of-payments position. There are no figures available for the net returns on private investment in the overseas provinces, but undoubtedly their loss would represent a severe shock to certain sectors of the business community. It is possible that prospective oil, power and mineral revenues will make Portuguese Africa more profitable in the future, but, when full account is taken of all costs, the provinces are not economically profitable to Portugal.

The costs of the war have mounted: between 1960 and 1970 the proportion of the GNP devoted to defence in metropolitan Portugal rose from 4 to 7 per cent, in Angola from 1 to 4 per cent, and from 1 to 3 per cent in Mozambique. The proportion of gross fixed capital investment devoted to defence rose from 20 to 40 per cent in metropolitan Portugal over the same decade, from 11 to 29 per cent in Angola, and from 14 to 28 per cent in Mozambique.

The absorption of such a high proportion of her financial resources in defence can logically only mean that Portugal has less to spend in other vital areas such as health, education and welfare. In comparison with the costs of defence, only 1.5 per cent of the GNP in metropolitan Portugal is devoted to education. It may be that the real cost of the war is being paid for in human terms. The government is aware of the implications of this: in a lecture to the senior defence college in Lisbon, the minister of finance argued that one of the tactics of the enemies of the regime was to force it to devote so much of its resources to defence that it might fail to satisfy 'the legitimate material satisfactions of the people', and concluded that it was vital that the government should dedicate 'an increasing percentage of our national resources to the satisfaction of the economic, social, cultural and spiritual aspirations of the people in order to reduce internal states of tension'.

It would appear that Portugal is able to bear the military and economic burdens of the defence effort almost indefinitely at its present level, and there seems to be little likelihood that any change of policy will be forced on her by external factors if she is determined to maintain that stand. The question is rather how far the defence effort will adversely affect the social and economic future of the home country. The Portuguese economy is at a vital stage in its evolution, and the regime has staked the country's future on its capacity to expand the economy. Yet Portugal is suffering from a labour shortage, and of the 120,000-150,000 troops in Africa, the majority are young men who would be better employed in the economic effort at home. Five years' military service means valuable time lost out of a working life and career. In terms of manpower the war absorbs a great deal of energy and talent which could be directed towards expansion of the home economy.

What will be Portugal's future relationship with the overseas provinces? Despite a certain war-weariness among the home population there is still no talk of abandonment of the provinces to the nationalists except from the extreme left-wing opposition. The majority of Portuguese support the government on Africa, but most of them would like to see an end to the war. The most desirable solution in the moderate view would be a federation of autonomous states, and the wording of certain clauses in the constitution has already been amended at government instigation in a manner which envisages the possibility of such a solution in the future.

Most Portuguese therefore do not contemplate a complete break with Africa in the foreseeable future; nor do they feel that there is a choice to be made between Africa and Europe. A public-opinion poll conducted in the summer of 1971 showed that while 54 per cent of the people questioned thought Portugal's entry into the EEC desirable, as many as 57 per cent believed that the future of the country depended primarily on the African provinces. Support for entry into the Common Market came primarily from business leaders, younger people, and the upper social classes. Significantly, however, of the businessmen interviewed, only 24 per cent thought it likely that Portugal would join within the next five years as against twice that number, 48 per cent, who felt it to be unlikely.

The concept 'Africa ends at the Pyrenees' still has some validity, even in the age of jet travel. Portugal is still a long way from Europe, her only land frontier is with Spain, not a member of the EEC, and between 85 per cent and 95 per cent of her trade is seaborne. With her African connections and the nature of her regime, close links with the European Community are unlikely in the near future. The older generation and the conservatives still cling to the idea of Portugal's ultramarine destiny, distrusting Europe. The younger, more forward-looking Portuguese would like to see a European future for their country, and look forward to the liberalization which a closer integration would bring.

Between the two, Caetano holds the balance, treading warily, keeping his own counsel. He is concerned with the future and with the past, anxious to modernize his country, yet fearful of losing what he considers to be her traditional values. The country he governs today is truly evolving, passing through a period of great change, full of contradictions yet equally of potentialities. There are challenges to be faced – emigration, industrialization, Africa, the EEC. But most important of all is Portugal's responsibility towards her own people; she must discover her future within her own boundaries – her destiny is no longer to be fulfilled abroad, but at home.

Notes on the text

1 THE INDIVIDUALITY OF PORTUGAL

1 Luís Vaz de Camões, *Sonetos*, No. 84, vol. I.
Ed. Hernâni Cidade, Lisbon, 1971 (4th edition).
2 George W. Ball, *The Disciple of Power*, Boston, 1968.
3 Pierre Birot, *Le Portugal*, Paris, 1950.

2 ROMANS, GOTHS AND MOORS

1 The Caliphate of Cordova was founded by 'Abdu'r-Rahman III in the early tenth century. It came to an end in 1031, and with it the unity it had imposed on the Muslims in the west. .

3 THE MARITIME ERA

1 Orlando Ribeiro, 'Formação de Portugal', in *Dicionário de História de Portugal*, vol. III, Lisbon, 1968.

4 THE GOLDEN AGE OF EMPIRE

1 Alexandre Herculano, *Opúsculos*, vol. VI. .

5 FOREIGN DOMINATION

1 English merchants or factors in foreign countries at that period formed associations known as 'Factories'. British traders in Lisbon and Oporto were known as 'merchants of the Factory' until 1810, when the Anglo-Portuguese Commercial Treaty abrogated the use of the term.

7 THE LIBERAL ERA

1 Alexandre Herculano, *Opúsculos*, vol. VII.
2 Iberianism, *Iberismo*, was the idea of union or federation of the two Iberian countries which gained considerable currency among liberal intellectuals during this period.

8 THE LIBERAL REPUBLIC 1910-1926

1 Using forged signatures on Bank of Portugal paper, a group of tricksters induced the British printing firm of Waterlow to print 580,000 500-escudo notes, with which they launched a bank. When the fraud was detected the Bank of Portugal sued Waterlow's, and a House of Lords judgement awarded the Bank £600,000 damages.

Select Bibliography

Livermore, H. V., *A New History of Portugal*, Cambridge, 1966.
(ed.) *Portugal and Brazil, an Introduction*, Oxford, 1953.
Kay, Hugh, *Salazar and Modern Portugal*, London, 1970.
Pattee, Richard, *Portugal and the Portuguese World*, Milwaukee, 1957.
Fryer, Peter, and Patricia McGowan Pinheiro, *Oldest Ally*, London, 1961.
Boxer, C. R., *The Portuguese Seaborne Empire 1415-1825*, London, 1969.
Abshire, D. M., and M. A. Samuels, *Portuguese Africa*, London, 1969.
Stanislawski, Dan, *The Individuality of Portugal*, Austin, Texas, 1959.
Xavier Pintado, V., *Structure and Growth of the Portuguese Economy*, EFTA, Geneva, 1964.
dos Santos, Reynaldo, *L'Art Portuguais*, Paris, 1953.
Smith, Robert C., *The Art of Portugal 1500-1800*, London, 1968.
Bradford, Sarah, *Portugal and Madeira*, London, 1969.
Bridge, Ann and Susan Lowndes, *The Selective Traveller in Portugal*, London, 1963.
Bradford, Sarah, *The Englishman's Wine, the Story of Port*, London, 1969.
Cheke, Marcus, *Dictator of Portugal, a life of the Marquis of Pombal*, London, 1938.
Cheke, Marcus, *Carlota Joaquina, Queen of Portugal*, London, 1947.
Gallop, Rodney, *Portugal, a Book of Folkways*, Cambridge, 1961.
Macaulay, Rose, *They Went to Portugal*, London, 1946.

Acknowledgments

Trustees of the British Museum, 8, 11; Graham Finlayson, 1, 2, 3, 5, 13, 23; Fotografia Artística Publicitária e Industrial Lda, 27; Mansell Collection, 16; Museu Nacional de Arte Antiga, Lisbon (courtesy, Direcção-Geral do Ensino Superior e das Belas-Artes, Ministerio da Educação Nacional), 6, 15; Secretario de Estado da Informação e Turismo, 7, 10, 17–22, 24–26, 28–30; Helga Schmidt-Glassner, 12, 14; Michael Teague, 9; Victoria and Albert Museum, London, 4.

Who's Who

AFONSO I, 'AFONSO HENRIQUES' (1109–85). First king of Portugal, founder of the kingdom and of the Burgundian dynasty. Son of Count Henry, cousin of the Duke of Burgundy and Teresa, illegitimate daughter of the King of Leon. Declared independence from the kingdom of Leon and won a large part of national territory including Lisbon from the Moors during his reign.

ALBUQUERQUE, AFONSO DE (1462–1515). The greatest figure in the history of Portugal's empire in the East. An able and just administrator, and a brilliant naval and military commander, he laid the foundations of Portuguese maritime hegemony in the Indian Ocean by securing the three key points of Ormuz, Goa and Malacca.

ALCOFORADO, MARIANA (1640–1723). A professed nun, she was the presumed authoress of the passionate *Letters of a Portuguese Nun*, which caused a European sensation when first published in Paris in 1669.

ALMADA NEGREIROS, JOSÉ DE (b. 1893). Gifted painter and poet, member of the avant garde group who collaborated in the magazine *Orpheu*.

CABRAL, PEDRO ALVARES DE (c. 1467–1520). Discovered Brazil, which he named Vera Cruz, en route for India in April 1500.

CAETANO, MARCELLO JOSÉ DAS NEVES (b. 1906). Appointed Prime Minister in 1968 after the illness of Salazar. A distinguished lawyer, he collaborated with Salazar in drafting the forms of the New State, is the author of several major works on administrative law and was rector of Lisbon University from 1959 to 1962.

CAMÕES, LUÍS VAZ DE (1517 or 1524–79). Portugal's greatest poet, author of *the Lusiads*, an epic centred on the voyage of Vasco da Gama which featured the heroic exploits of the Portuguese throughout their history. A disciple of the Renaissance, he recreated the Portuguese language in his *Sonnets*, which represent the ultimate in Portuguese lyric verse.

CARLOS I (1890–1908). Penultimate king of the Bragança dynasty, his attempt to end the farcical rotativist system with the dictatorship of João Franco led indirectly to his assassination in 1908.

CASTELO BRANCO, CAMILO (1825–90). Romantic novelist whose books depicted rural life. Committed suicide in 1890.

CASTRO, INÊS PIRES DE (d. 1355). Heroine of a famous tragic royal love story which has inspired countless plays and novels, she was the Galician mistress of Pedro I when he was heir to the throne, and was murdered on his father's orders.

CASTRO, Dom JOÃO DE (1500–48). Viceroy of India during the golden age of Portugal's eastern empire. An incorruptible administrator and brave soldier, he was also author of three *Roteiros*, navigational handbooks of the Red Sea and Indian coasts.

CASTRO, JOSÉ MARIA FERREIRA DE (b. 1898). Major modern novelist who became internationally known with the publication of *A Selva* in 1923.

CEREJEIRA, Dom MANUEL GONÇALVES (b. 1888). Contemporary and close friend of Salazar at Coimbra University and throughout his life, he became Cardinal Patriarch of Lisbon in 1930 and retired in 1971.

CORTESÃO, JAIME (1884–1960). Leading historian and intellectual figure of the Republican era. Founded the influential liberal review *Seara Nova*, and went into exile in 1927 for his part in an attempt to oust the military junta of 1926. Remained in exile for thirty years, during which time he wrote his major historical works.

COSTA, AFONSO AUGUSTO DA (1871–1937). As minister of Justice in the first provisional government of the Republic in 1910 he was responsible for drastic legislation disestablishing the Church and legalizing divorce. Leader of the Democratic party and four times head of the government, he was among the most radical and anti-clerical of the republican politicians.

DELGADO, HUMBERTO (1906-65). Former Salazar supporter who became an opposition leader during the 1950's. Presented himself as candidate in the 1958 presidential election, and afterwards went into exile. Murdered near Badajoz in 1965.

DINÍS I (1279–1325). Called 'The Farmer', he was one of the most remarkable kings of the Burgundian dynasty, a gifted administrator who encouraged commerce, fostered agriculture and founded the first Portuguese university in 1290. He was also a poet and made his court a cultural centre.

FRANCO NOGUEIRA, ALBERTO (b. 1918). One of Salazar's most brilliant ministers, and apologist for the Portuguese position in Africa. As Foreign Minister from 1961 Franco Nogueira bore the brunt of anticolonialist attacks on Portuguese policy. He left the government in 1969, and is now spokesman for the extreme right wing.

GAMA, VASCO DA (1468–1524). Admiral of the fleet which made the historic first sea passage to India, landing at Calicut in 1498. Da Gama was made Conde de Vidigueira and Viceroy of India, and died at Cochin.

GARRETT, JOÃO BAPTISTA DE ALMEIDA (1799–1854). Leading literary and political figure of the early liberal era, he introduced the Romantic movement and founded the modern Portuguese theatre. His best-known play is *Frei Luís de Sousa*.

GÓIS, DAMIÃO DE (1502–74). Humanist, author, historian and companion of Erasmus, de Góis travelled Europe and returned to Portugal during the brief flowering of humanism under João III. His fate illustrated the sad destiny of Portuguese humanism: persecuted by the Inquisition, he retired from the court and died, probably murdered, in 1574.

GONÇALVES, NUNO (active mid-fifteenth century). The greatest painter Portugal has produced, author of the fifteenth-century masterpiece the *Panels of St Vincent*.

HENRY THE NAVIGATOR (1394–1460). Fifth child of João I and his English queen, Philippa of Lancaster, he was the inspiration of the early voyages of discovery, which he financed and organized.

HERCULANO, ALEXANDRE DE CARVALHO ARAÚJO (1810–77). Leading liberal intellectual and historian. Although he retired from public life he remained the most influential figure of his age. An anti-clerical and a fighter for social justice, he wrote a monumental *History of Portugal* and his works on public issues such as education and emigration were classics.

JOÃO I (1385–1433). The bastard son of Pedro I, he became one of the leaders of the popular revolt against the Spanish-oriented government in 1383, and became first king of the Aviz dynasty – so called from his title of Master of the Order of Aviz. He married Philippa of Lancaster, daughter of John of Gaunt, and his capture of Ceuta in 1415 was Portugal's first territorial conquest overseas.

JOÃO II (1455–96). Called the Perfect Prince for his exceptional qualities, he was one of the most remarkable kings in Portuguese history. He played a principal part in the foundation of Portugal's maritime empire in the East, and centralized and strengthened royal power at home.

JOÃO IV (1603–1656). First king of the Bragança dynasty, the former Duke of Bragança descended from a bastard son of João I. He came to the throne when the independence revolt of 1640 expelled the Spaniards. His daughter Catherine of Bragança married Charles II of England.

JOÃO V (1707–50). Intelligent and cultivated sovereign whose long reign represented an artistic renaissance founded on the wealth which the Crown derived from the gold and diamond mines of Brazil. After a brilliant beginning, decline set in with the king's protracted illness and government stagnated in the hands of churchmen.

MAGELLAN or MAGALHÃES, FERNÃO DE (c. 1480–1521). Initiator of the historic first circumnavigation of the globe, undertaken under the patronage of the King of Spain, Magellan having quarrelled with Manuel I. The fleet of five ships and 250 men left Spain in September 1519 and returned in September 1522 with only one ship and eighteen men, Magellan himself having been killed in a skirmish in the Philippines in 1521.

MANUEL I (1469–1521). Called the Fortunate, since the Portuguese empire in the East was at its height under his rule. Culturally also his reign was one of the great periods of Portuguese history. He introduced the bureaucratic and mercantilist state, strengthening the royal power against baronial and municipal privileges, and issued the decree which resulted in the forcible conversion of the Portuguese Jews.

MARTINS, JOAQUIM PEDRO DE OLIVEIRA (1845–94). Liberal polemicist and historian, author of a History of Iberian Civilization and a History of Portugal. A fervent advocate of Iberian federalism, he was a member of the short-lived group of liberal intellectuals called the Vencidos da Vida.

MELO, Dom FRANCISCO MANUEL DE (1608–66). One of the principal literary figures of the seventeenth century, poet, playwright, courtier and apologist for the Bragança restoration; author of a *Handbook for Husbands*.

PAIS, SIDÓNIO BERNARDINO CARDOSO DA SILVA (1872–1918). Leader of a successful coup against the radical Democratic government of Afonso Costa in 1917. He believed in a presidential system of government and governed as a dictator for one year until his assassination.

PEREIRA, Dom NUNO ÁLVARES (1360–1431). Called the Holy Constable, he was a brilliant military leader who played a major part in the revolution of 1383, and later joined the Carmelite Order.

PESSOA, FERNANDO ANTÓNIO NOGUEIRA (1888–1935). Poet of genius and one of the most complex literary personalities of the twentieth century. Leader of the modern movement in Portugal and founder of the avant garde review, *Orpheu*.

PHILIPPA OF LANCASTER (1360–1415). English queen of João I, she was the eldest daughter of John of Gaunt and Blanche of Lancaster, and mother of the 'illustrious generation' of princes which included Henry the Navigator.

POMBAL, SEBASTIÃO JOSÉ DE CARVALHO E MELO, MARQUIS OF (1699–1782). Dictator of Portugal as Prime Minister under José I (1750–77). A controversial figure, the motive force of the harshest government Portugal had known, he instigated the rebuilding of Lisbon after the disastrous earthquake of 1755, curbed the pretensions of the great nobility, expelled the Jesuits, reformed education and promoted Portuguese industry.

QUEIRÓS, EÇA DE (1845–1900). Portugal's greatest novelist, whose books mirror the society of his day, he was also a liberal intellectual of the 'generation of '70' and the *Vida Nova*. After making an aristocratic marriage he lost his early passionate interest in politics and even his anticlericalism, and became steadily more right-wing. As a novelist his style, wit and powers of observation put him in a class of his own. Among his best-known books which have been translated into English are: *The Maias*, *The City and the Mountains*, *The Relic*, and *The Sin of Father Amaro*.

QUENTAL, ANTERO TARQUÍNIO DE (1842–91). Major poet and committed liberal idealist, Antero was the inspiration of the *Cenáculo*, followers of

Proudhon who included Eça de Queirós and Oliveira Martins. He also organized the *Conferências Democráticas*, advocating a republican peninsular federation and socialism. Subject to grave melancholia, he destroyed his political programme and retired to a provincial town to write his *Sonnets*. A brief return to public life at the time of the Ultimatum ended in disaster and he committed suicide in his native island of São Miguel in the Azores.

RODRIGUES, AMÁLIA (b. 1920). Known simply as 'Amália', a legend in her own country and internationally famous, she is the greatest fado singer of all time.

SALAZAR, ANTÓNIO DE OLIVEIRA (1889–1970). Prime Minister and virtual ruler of Portugal from 1932 to 1968, Salazar was first brought into the government as Finance Minister in 1928 by the military junta which overthrew the Republic in 1926. A professor of Economics at Coimbra University, he rescued Portugal's wavering economy in the 1920's, and created the Estado Novo, the corporative state which remains the political system today. He suffered a severe stroke in 1968 which incapacitated him, and he was replaced as Prime Minister by Professor Marcello Caetano.

SEBASTIÃO I (1554–78). Penultimate king of the Aviz dynasty. His reckless expedition into Morocco culminated in the disastrous battle of al-Ksar el-Kebir, and led directly to the extinction of the dynasty and the annexation of Portugal by Philip II of Spain. A messianic cult, Sebastianism, grew up round the myth that he had not been killed in the battle and would return to lead his country to glory and independence.

SÉRGIO, ANTÓNIO (1883–1968). Minister of Education in the Texeira Gomes government of 1923, Sérgio was a leading intellectual of the liberal *Seara Nova* group, author, man of letters and outspoken critic of the Salazar régime.

SILVEIRA, JOSÉ XAVIER MOUZINHO DA (1780–1849). One of the key figures of the early liberal period. As Minister of Justice and the Treasury (1832–3) Mouzinho was responsible for the first great body of reforming and innovatory legislation which laid the foundations of the new state. He made many enemies and eventually retired, disillusioned, from public life.

TOMÁS, AMÉRICO DEUS RODRIGUES (b. 1894). Distinguished naval officer who became Minister of the Marine under Salazar and recreated the merchant navy after World War II. Elected President of the Republic in 1958 and re-elected in 1965 and 1972.

VICENTE, GIL (c. 1465–c. 1536). Portugal's first and greatest playwright, he wrote verse plays in the vernacular which were unique for his time and represented a bridge between the Middle Ages and the Renaissance. He was also a talented goldsmith whose masterpiece is the Belém Monstrance.

VIEIRA, PADRE ANTÓNIO (1608–97). Brilliant preacher, model prose writer, missionary and fighter for human rights, Vieira was one of the most quixotic and colourful figures of the Restoration period.

VIEIRA DA SILVA, MARIA HELENA (b. 1908). The most talented contemporary Portuguese artist; internationally known, she lives in Paris.

Index

Page numbers in italic refer to illustrations

Acção Nacional Popular, 88, 93
administration, national and
    colonial, 54
adultery, 140
Afonso I (see Who's Who, p.162),
    12, 28, 30
Afonso III, 30, 33
Afonso V, 36, 37
Afonso, Jorge, 41
Africa, Portuguese presence in, 49,
    70–1, 76, 82, 86–7, 91, 122 *ff.*,
    155–7; costs of, 156–7; *see also*
    anti-colonialism *and under*
    individual colonies
agriculture *see* farming
Águas Livres aqueduct, 53
Albuquerque, Afonso de (see
    Who's Who, p. 162), 38, 46,
    61
Alcácer, 26
Alcobaça, 16, 29
Alcoforado, Soror Mariana (see
    Who's Who, p. 162), 140
Alentejo, 18; irrigation scheme,
    103, 104, 126–7
Alfeizerão, 138
Alfonso VI of Leon, 27–8
Alfonso VII of Castile and Leon,
    28
Algarve, 11, 19, 27, 28
al-Idrisī, 15, 28
Aljubarrota, 16, 33, 124
al-Ksar el-Kebir, battle of, 48, 49
Almada Megreiros, José de (see
    Who's Who, p. 162)
Almeida, António José de, 74
Alto Douro, 14, 15
Alva, Duke of, 49
Alvão, Serra de, 10
Amado, Jorge, 148

Amarante, 138
Amboina, 39
Andressen, Sofia de Mello
    Breyner, 141, 147
Anglo-Portuguese Alliance, 34,
    51, 54, 71, 82, 124–5
Angola, 19, 71, 86, 108, 109; and
    African nationalism, 131, 155–7;
    and the slave trade, 39;
    Portuguese attitude towards,
    122
anti-colonialism, 86–7, 125, 127;
    African, 131–3, 155–7
Arabia, 39
Arabs, 16, 25–7
architecture, 14, 26; Baroque, 53;
    Manueline, 40, *62*, *63*;
    Renaissance, 40; Romanesque,
    29
Arguim, 49
army, the, as a force in politics, 94
Arruda, Diogo and Francisco de,
    40
Art of Being Portuguese, The
    (Pascoães), 137
arts, 40–1
Augustus, 24
Aveiro, 15
Aviz, Order of, 33
Azores, the, 19, 20, 35, 83; base
    agreement, 121, 127
Azurara, Gomes Eanes de, 34

bacalhau, 137–8
Bairrada, 15
Bakunin, Ivan, 134
balance of payments, 101, 102
Banco do Fomento, 84, 107
Banda, 39
Banda, Dr Hastings, 131

Bandung Conference, 86
bank-note scandal (1925), 77
Baroque, 53
Barreiro, 17
Barros, João de, 42
Batalha, 16, 40, *63*
Beatriz, 33
Beckford, William, 138
Beira (Mozambique), 125, 132
Beira Alta, 11, 14
Beja, 28, 86
Belém, 40, 41, *62*; custard tarts,
    138; Monstrance, 41
Benfica, 145–6
Beresford, Lord, 66
Bessa Luís, Agustina, 141, 148
biscato, 137
Bojador, Cape, 35
Boytac, Jean, 40
Braga, 12, 25, 28
Braga, Teófilo, 74
brasileiros, 128
Brazil, 20, 39, 45, 46, 49, 55, 65,
    66, 122; secession of, 66–7;
    special relationship with, 127–9
British Ultimatum (1890), 70, 71
Bruges, 32
Buchanan, George, 43
bull-breeding, 17
bullfighting, 146
business interests, 95–6

CABORA BASSA dam, 126, 132, 156
Cabral, Amilcar, 155
Cabral, Pedro Alvares de (*see*
    Who's Who, p. 162), 39
Caetano, Marcello (*see* Who's
    Who, p. 162), 23, 89, 90 *ff.*, *114*,
    149–51, 158; and Africa, 121; on
    Brazil, 128–9; political
    programme of, 93; reforms of,
    98–9; views on emigration, 111
cafés, 139
Caixa Geral de Depósitos, 107
cakes, 138
Calatrava, Order of, 29
Calicut, 36
Camacho, Brito, 74

Câmara Corporativa, 89–90
Cambay, 39
Camões, Luis de (*see* Who's Who,
    p. 162), 21, 34, 37, 41, 42, 48
campinos, 17, *117*
canning industry, 105
Cape Verde islands, 19, 123
caravels, 26, *58*
Carbonária, the, 71
Cardoso Pires, José, 148
Carlos I (*see* Who's Who, p. 163),
    71
Carlos, Frei, 41
cartography, 41, *60–1*
Casa da Índia, 39
Castelo Branco, Camilo (*see*
    Who's Who, p. 163), 72, 148
castiços, 52
Castillo, Juan de, 40
Castro, Ferreira de, 148
Castro, Inês de (*see* Who's Who,
    p. 163), 131
Castro, Dom João de (*see* Who's
    Who, p. 163), 46
Castro, José Maria Ferreira de (*see*
    Who's Who, p. 163)
castros, 24, 25
Catherine of Bragança, 138
censorship, 55, 75, 92, 93, 98–9
Cerejeira, Dom Manuel
    Gonçalves, Cardinal (*see* Who's
    Who, p. 163), 95
Ceuta, 35
Ceylon, 39
Chanterene, Nicholas, 40–1
Chaves, 14
China, 39
Christ, Order of, 35, 40
Church, the, 43–4, 47, 65, 69, 71,
    74, 75, 143–4; and social
    involvement, 144–5; Caetano
    and, 95; disestablishment, 144;
    Salazar and, 81–2, 95; *see also*
    Counter-Reformation,
    Inquisition, Jesuits
Cistercians, 16, 29
City and the Mountains, The
    (Queirós), 126

Coimbra, 15, 28, 29, 33; art and
architecture in, 41; University,
43, 53, 56, 115
Common Market, 93, 102, 108,
109, 121, 125–6, 158
communications, 15, 24, 31–2, 68
communism, 82, 85, 91, 92, 96,
123, 127
compadres, 142–3
Companhia União Fabril, 95
concelhos, 33
Concordat (1940), 82, 95
Conimbriga, 25
Constitution (1820), 66; (1933),
80–1, 88
Constitutional Charter (1826), 66
COREMO (Mozambican
nationalists), 156
Coromandel, 39
Corporate Chamber, 89–90
corporate state, 19, 91, 149; see
also Estado Novo
Corrêa, Gaspar, 42
cortes, 33, 44–5, 67; see also
National Assembly
Cortesão, Jaime (see Who's Who,
p. 163), 77
Costa, Afonso (see Who's Who,
p. 163), 74, 75
Costa, Gen. Gomes da, 77
Costa, João da, 43
cost of living, 137
Council of State, 88
Counter-Reformation, the, 42–4,
48, 130
Courses in Christianity, 144
courting, 140
Couto, Diogo de, 42
coutos de homiziados, 29
Cova da Beira, 15
Covadonga, 27
Covilhã, Pero de, 22, 36
Cunha, Dom Luís da, 55
cunhas, 142–3
currency, strength of the, 84

DAMÃO, 20, 124
de Gaulle, General Charles, 126

Delgado, General Humberto (see
Who's Who, p. 163), 86
democratization, 150
Development Plans see under
Second, Third
DGS (Direcção Geral de
Segurança) see PIDE
diamond mining, 53, 128
Dias, Bartolomeu, 36
Dinís, 32, 33
discovery see exploration
Diu, 20, 124
divorce, 95
doctors, 153
donations, the, 18, 29, 67, 102
Douro, 10, 11
drunkenness, 138

EANES, Gil, 35
education, 55, 56, 69, 72, 78, 93,
140, 150–1, 157; liberal reforms,
140–1
Edward III of England, 33
EEC see Common Market
elections, 92, 97
el-Mina, 49
Elvas, 18
emigrants and emigration, 12, 14,
18, 46, 69, 92, 110–11, 152; from
the land to the cities, 136–7, 152;
to Brazil, 53, 110, 128
English in Portugal, 51, 108, 124–5
Enlightenment, Age of the, 55
escudo area, the, 109
Espinheiro monastery, 41
Estado da Índia, 38
Estado Novo (Salazar), 69, 80–1, 88
Estado Social (Caetano), 93
estrangeirados, 52, 53, 55, 148
Estremadura, 15–16, 29
Estremoz, 18
Ethiopia, 36
eucalyptus, 19, 104
European Free Trade Association
(EFTA), 125–6
Évora, 25, 28, 29, 33; art and
architecture in, 41
exploration, 34 ff., 60–1

fado, 146–7
family allowances, 154
family relationships, 142
Faria, Severim de, 110
farming, 15, 18, 26, 46, 101 *ff.*,
    116–17, 154; conservatism of,
    103, 135; defects of, 102;
    modernization of, 104
Faro, 11, 26, 28
Fátima, 16, 81, *114*, 143, 144
feitorias, 35, 38, 45
Fernandes, Garcia, 41
Fernandes, Vasco ('Grão Vasco'),
    41
Fernando I, 32, 33
Ferreira, Vergílio, 148
Figueiredo, Antero de, 144
Figueiredo, Cristovão de, 41
fishing, 14, 15, 26, 105, *116*, 154
flora, 11–12, 16
food, 137–9
football, 145–6
foreign investment, 124, 126–7,
    131
Franco Nogueira, Alberto (*see*
    Who's Who, p. 164), 123, 131,
    143
freemasonry, 65–6, 71
FRELIMO (Mozambican
    nationalists), 86, 156
Freyre, Gilberto, 122

GAMA, Vasco da (*see* Who's Who,
    p. 164), 22, 36, 41, 42, *61*
Garrett, João Baptista de Almeida
    (*see* Who's Who, p. 164), 67, 68,
    72
'generation of '70', the, 69
Goa, 20, 38, 46, 49; annexation of,
    86, 124
Gois, Damião de (*see* Who's Who,
    p. 164), 43
gold, 35, 39, 49, 53, 128
gold standard, 72, 80
Gonçalves, Antão, 35
Gonçalves, Nuno (*see* Who's
    Who, p. 164), 37, 41
Goths, 25

Gouveia, André de, 43
Guarda, 14, 15
Guimarães, 12, 28
Guiné (Portuguese Guinea), 19,
    39, 86; African nationalism in,
    131–2, 155
Gusmão, Alexandre de, 53–4

'HANDBOOK FOR HUSBANDS' (de
    Melo), 139
Hanseatic League, 32
harbours, 32
health insurance, 153–4
Henrique, Cardinal, 48
Henry of Burgundy, 28
Henry the Navigator, Prince (*see*
    Who's Who, p. 164), 22, 34, 35,
    36, 37, 59
Herculano, Alexandre (*see* Who's
    Who, p. 164), 21, 47, 68–9, 72,
    110
herdades, 18, 25
Históricos, 68
History of Portugal (Herculano), 69
History of the Inquisition
    (Herculano), 69
Holy Office *see* Inquisition
Homem de Mello, Pedro, 147
Hospitallers, 29
housing, 152–3
humanist movement, the, 43

IBERIANISM, 69, 129: see also *Pacto
    Iberico*
Iberian peninsula, 9
illiteracy, 150–1
income *per capita*, 101, 134
industry, 84–5, 101 *ff.*; foreign
    investment in, 107, 124, 126–7,
    131; rationalization of, 106;
    state participation in, 107
infant mortality rates, 153
inflation, 76–7, 85, 112, 137
Inquisition, the, 43–4, 51, 55, 130
insurance, marine, 34
international relations, 121 *ff.*
irrigation, 19, 26, 103

Isabel, Saint, 140
Ivory Coast, 132

JAPAN, 39, 45, 49, 61; trade with,
    109
Jesuits, 43, 45, 49, 51, 55;
    expulsion of, 55, 56
Jews, 14, 35, 37; persecution of, 43
Joana, Saint, 140
João I (see Who's Who, p. 165),
    16, 33, 59, 124
João II (see Who's Who, p. 165),
    36, 45
João III, 39, 40, 42–4, 45
João IV (see Who's Who, p. 165),
    50, 51
João V (see Who's Who, p. 165),
    53, 54, 55, 128
João VI, 66
José I, 55
Juan I of Castile, 33
Junqueiro, Guerra, 72

LABOUR, Statute of, 141
Lamas, Maria, 148
land distribution, 102–3
latifundia, 18, 25, 102
Latin American free trade
    association (LAFTA), 129
law and order, 98, 99
Legião Portuguesa, 81
legistas, 33
Leiria, 32; Cortes of, 33
Leitura Nova, 41
Leixões, 15
Lendas da Índia (Corrêa), 42
Leonor, Queen, 33
letrados, 33, 50
Letters of a Portuguese Nun
    (Alcoforado), 140
lezirias, 17, 18
liberalism, 68–9, 72, 97, 149
life expectancy, 153
Lins do Rego, José, 148
Lisbon, 11, 16–17, 26, 29, 30, 33,
    65, 137; art and architecture in,
    41; University of, 74, 91;
    harbour, 106

LISNAVE, 106, 119
literature, 41–2, 72
    contemporary, 147–8
Livingstone, David, 70
Lobo, Maria Teresa, 141
Lopes, Fernão, 32
Lopes, Gregório, 41
López Rodó, Laureano, 130
lottery, 120, 144
Louis XIV, 51
Luanda, 155
Ludwig or Ludovice, 53
Lusiads, The (Camões), 42
Lusitania, 24–5
Luso-Brazilian Community,
    127–9
luso-tropicalism, 122

MACAU, 20, 38, 45
Machado, Bernardino, 74
Madariaga, Salvador de, 20
Madeira, 19, 20, 35, 39;
    honey cakes, 138
Mafra, 53
Magellan, Fernão de (see Who's
    Who, p. 165), 22
Maias, The (de Queirós), 17, 22,
    146
Malacca, 38, 49
Malawi, 131
Manuel I (see Who's Who, p. 165),
    36, 38, 40, 44
manufacturing, 105–6
Margueira, 17
Maria da Glória (Maria II), 66
Martins, Joaquim Pedro de
    Oliveira (see Who's Who,
    p. 165), 69
Martins, Rogério, 93
Matosinhos, 15
Melo, Dom Francisco Manuel de
    (see Who's Who, p. 166), 139
Mendes Pinto, Fernão, 22, 42
Mértola, 26
Miguel, Dom, 66
military service, 18, 111, 136, 157
Minho, 10, 11, 12, 14
minifundia, 12, 102

Miranda, Sá de, 42, 110
Miranda do Douro, 14
Mocidade Portuguesa, 81
Monção, 14
Mondego, river, 15, 28
Mondlane, Eduardo, 86
Monomotapa, 39
montes, 25
Moors, 19, 25–7
Moreira, Adriano, 143
Morocco, 35, 36, 45
Mourão Ferreira, David, 147
Movimento de Unidade Democrático
   (MUD), 85
Movimento Nacional Democrático
   (MND), 85
Movimento Nacional Feminino, 81
Mozambique, 19, 82, 86, 109, 123,
   126; and African nationalism,
   131–2, 155, 156, 157
Mozarabs, 29, 30
MPLA, 155
Muslims, 15–16, 25–7, 34–5;
   trading in the East, 38, 39

NAMORA, Fernando, 148
National Assembly, 89, 94, 97
navigation, see seafaring
Nazzoni or Nasoni, 53
Nehru, Pandit Jawaharlal, 86
Neto, Agostinho, 155
neutrality, 54, 76, 82, 83, 84, 124
'New Christians', 44, 45, 51, 55,
   130
New State, see Estado Novo
Nixon, Richard M., 121
North Atlantic Treaty
   Organization (NATO), 84, 86,
   121, 125, 127, 155

OLD-AGE PENSIONS, 154
'Old Christians', 55
olive growing, 18, 26
O'Neill, Alexandre, 147
Oporto, 14–15, 16, 28, 33, 65;
   siege of, 68; University of, 74
opposition, political, 85–6, 87, 92,
   96–7

Opus Dei, 95, 130
Organization of African Unity
   (OAU), 131
Ormuz, 38, 39, 49
Orpheu, 147
Ortigão, Ramalho, 70
Ourém, Conde de, 33
Ourique, battle of, 28
overseas territories, 19

Pacto Iberico, 82, 130
PAIGC (Guiné nationalists), 155
painting, 41
Pais, Álvaro, 33
Pais, Sidónio (see Who's Who,
   p. 166), 75
Palmela, 29
Panels of St Vincent (Gonçalves), 37
Pascoães, Teixeira de, 137
Passos Manuel, 67, 69
pastry shops, 138
Pedro I, 33, 131
Pedro, Dom, 66
Pelayo of Asturias, 27
pepper, 39, 46
Peregrinação (Mendes Pinto), 42
Pereira, Dom Nuno Álvares (see
   Who's Who, p. 166)
Pereira de Moura, Francisco, 97
Peres, Vimara, 27
Persia, 39, 49
personal relationships, 142–3
Pessagna, Emmanuele, 32
Pessoa, Fernando (see Who's Who,
   p. 166), 147
Philip II of Spain, 48
Philippa of Lancaster (see Who's
   Who, p. 166), 34, 59
physical geography, 10–11, 20
PIDE, 81, 93, 98
pig-killing, 135
pilgrimages, 143
Pinhal do Rei, 32
Pintado, Valentin Xavier, 93, 103
pirates, 32
poetry, 42, 147
political change, 150
Pombal, Marquis of (see Who's

Who, p. 166), 55–6, *64*
Pompidou, Georges, 121
population, 12, 20, 46, 65, 70, 104, 136
Portucale, 27–8
Portuguese Guinea, *see* Guiné
port wine, 14, 15, 124
PRAGMA, 97
presidency, the, 75, 90, 150
Prester, John, 36
prime minister, power of the, 88–9
Principe, 19
Proença, Raul, 77
Progressistas, 68
Puritanos, 55

QUEIRÓS, Eça de (*see* Who's Who, p. 166), 17, 69, 70, 72, 126, 139, 146, 148
Quental, Antero de (*see* Who's Who, p. 166), 69, 72

RAINFALL, 11
Rau, Virginia, 141
Real Academia da História, 53
Real Mesa da Censura, 55, 56
Reconquest, the, 15, 18, 27–30, 122, 130
Regeneradores, 67–8
religion, 16, 27, 43–4, 74, 81
republicanism, 70–1, 73 *ff.*
Republican party, the, 70, 71, 73
Revolution (1910), 73–4
Rhodesia, 125, 132
Ribatejo, 17–18
Ribeiro, Aquilino, 148
Ribeiro, Bernardim, 42
roads, 24
Rodrigues, Amália (*see* Who's Who, p. 167), 147
Roman Empire, 24–5
'Rose-coloured map', the, 70–1
Rouen, Jean de, 40

SÁ CARNEIRO, Mário de, 147
Sahara, the, 35
Salazar, António de Oliveira (*see* Who's Who, p. 167), 21–2, 69,

79–83, 90, *114*, 126, 143; and education, 151; and Franco, 82, 130; and the Church, 95; economic theories, 80, 107; last years of, 86–7
Salazar bridge, 17, *113*, 126
Salgueiro, João, 93, 97
Salisbury, Marquess of, 71
Santa Maria hijacking, 86
Santiago, Knights of, 29
Santos, Machado, 76
São Paulo, 128
São Tomé, 19, 39
sardine fishing, 105, *116–17*
saudades, 21
sculpture, 40–1
seafaring, 31 *ff.*; source of artistic motifs, 40; *see also* exploration
Seara Nova group, 77
Sebastianism, 49–50
Sebastião I (*see* Who's Who, p. 167), 48, 49
Second Development Plan, 84, 104
SEDES (Society for Economic and Social Development), 93, 97, 99, 150
Seixal, 17
Senegal, 35
Senegambia, 35
Sergio, António (*see* Who's Who, p. 167), 77
Serpa, 18
Serpa Pinto, Alexandre de, 71
Serra da Estrêla, 15
Setúbal, 18
Severa, Maria, 146
shipbuilding, 26, 32, 106
Siderurgia Nacional, 17, 106
Silva, Antonio José da, 44
Silva, Duarte da, 44
Silveira, José Xavier Mouzinho da (*see* Who's Who, p. 167), 67
silver, 48–9
Silves, 26
Simão, José Veiga, 93, 151
Sinédrio, 66
Sines, 107

Sintra, 26
slave trade, 35, 39, 45, 49, 51, 55
smuggling, 55
Socialist party, the, 70
social security and welfare, 153–4
society and social questions, 46–7,
  50–2, 65, 134 ff.; see also
  emigration, population
Sofala, 38, 45
South Africa, relations with, 132
Spain, period of domination by,
  48–50; civil war, 82;
  relationship with, 129–31
spice trade, 36, 38, 39
Stanley, H. M., 70
Strabo, 24
strikes, 75, 76, 81, 99
student unrest, 85, 141–2, 151
Suez Canal, 17
suffrage, 75, 92; female, 141
sugar trade, 39, 45, 46,˙49, 128
Swabians, 12, 16, 25

Tagus (Tejo), 11, 32
technical training, 151
Teivo, Diogo de, 43
Templars, 29
Ternate, 38, 39
Third Development Plan, 19, 104,
  153
Tidore, 39
Timor, 20
Tomar, 18, 29, 40, 62
Tomás, Admiral Américo (see
  Who's Who, p. 167), 86, 90
Tordesillas, Treaty of, 36
Torga, Miguel, 148
Torralva, Diogo de, 40
tourism, 109–10
trade and commerce, 32, 35–7,
  38–9, 45, 49; with Brazil, 55
trade unions, 92, 96
Tragic History of the Sea, 42

Trás-os-Montes, 10, 11, 14
tuberculosis, 153

Ultramar, 19
União Nacional, 81, 92; see also
  Acção Nacional Popular
Union of the Two Crowns, 49
UNITA (Mozambican
  nationalists), 156
United Nations, 86–7, 130
University Catholic Youth, 144
UPA, 155
Upper Niger, 35

Vaz Dourado, Fernão, 41
Vencidos da Vida, 70
Verdadeiro Metodo de Estudar
  (Verney), 54, 56
Verde, Cesário, 21, 72
Verney, Luís António, 54, 56
Viana do Castelo, 11, 14, 103
Vicente, Gil (see Who's Who,
  p. 168), 41, 42, 137
Vieira, Padre António (see Who's
  Who, p. 168), 50
Vieira da Silva, Maria Helena (see
  Who's Who, p. 168), 141
Vila Nova de Gaia, 15
vinho verde, 14
Viriatus, 24
Viseu, 41, 103
Visigoths, 25, 27
vital statistics, 153
Vouga, river, 15

War of the two brothers
  (1832–34), 65, 66
Windsor, Treaty of, 34, 124
wine, 14, 15, 25, 116
women, attitude towards, 139–41;
  discrimination against, 141
women's liberation, 141
World War I, 76

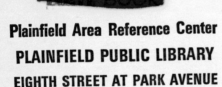